I0136128

Introduction

Let's take a step back in time, with no DeLorean needed. Whether you remember sock hops, soda fountains, Woodstock, or the dawn of video games, this book is your invitation to relive the magic.

This collection spans the 1940s through the 1990s, with a special focus on the decades that defined so many memories: the 50s, 60s, 70s, and 80s. Inside, you'll find a mix of easy favorites and more challenging "**Wait, was it that?**" curveballs from music, movies, pop culture, headline news, sports, fashion and more.

WHAT YOU'LL FIND INSIDE

- 500 trivia questions divided by decade.

- Flashback Facts: short bursts of nostalgia tucked in every few pages to spark conversations and those "Oh wow, I remember that!" moments.

- Answers for each decade at the back of the book to see how well you did. When you finish a section, tally your score and see where you land. Some decades have more questions than others, so the scoring is adjusted to keep it fair.

Grade Yourself

FOR SECTIONS WITH 90-100 QUESTIONS ('50S-'80S)

90–100: **Trivia Titan**
70–89: **Nostalgia Buff**
50–69: **Memory Keeper**
30–49: **Flashback Fan**
Below 30: **Time Traveler in Training**

FOR SECTIONS WITH 30 QUESTIONS ('40S & '90S)

25–30: **Decade Dominator**
15–24: **Nostalgia Buff**
10–14: **Memory Keeper**
5–9: **Flashback Fan**
Below 5: **Retro Rookie**

Play solo, challenge family and friends, or skip the scoring altogether and just enjoy the memories. **No rules required!** Grab a pen or pencil, start with your favorite decade, and get ready to laugh, reminisce, and test how much you really remember!

The Swinging '40s

The 1940s were a whirlwind of big bands, big movies, and big changes. Families gathered around the radio for comedy shows and breaking news, ration books lived in kitchen drawers, and swing music kept spirits high. Kids stacked Tinkertoy sets, movie lovers swooned over Casablanca, and a fun new vehicle stole the spotlight: the Jeep. By the time peace arrived, people were jitterbugging in dance halls, grilling hot dogs in the backyard, and lining up for ice cream floats. It was a decade of hope and plenty of good times, so polish your shoes, turn up Glenn Miller, and get ready to roll into the '40s!

FLASHBACK FACT

Victory gardens were small vegetable gardens planted by families during World War II to support the war effort. They weren't just patriotic; they were practical too. At their peak, these backyard plots produced almost 40% of all vegetables grown in the U.S.

1   Who became the breakout star of late-1940s television, earning the unforgettable nickname "Mr. Television"?

    a) Bob Hope   c) Milton Berle
    b) Groucho Marx   d) Sid Caesar

2   The Andrews Sisters had everyone singing along with their catchy hit "Rum and _____."

    a) Beer   c) Root Beer
    b) Coca-Cola   d) Lemonade

3   Which 1942 wartime film starred Humphrey Bogart as Rick Blaine, owner of a nightclub in French Morocco?

    a) Citizen Kane   c) Casablanca
    b) It's a Wonderful Life   d) The Maltese Falcon

4 Which classic mystery board game, released in 1949, let families accuse Professor Plum in the library with the candlestick?

a) Monopoly

c) Clue

b) Stratego

d) Sorry!

5 If you were jitterbugging in the dance halls of the 1940s, what kind of music kept your feet flying?

a) Soul

c) Swing

b) Blues

d) Doo-wop

6 Before he was part of the Marvel Cinematic Universe, this shield-wielding Super-Soldier made his explosive, highly patriotic debut in 1941 for Timely Comics (pre-dating the Avengers by decades!)–who is this red, white, and blue hero?

a) Superman

c) Captain America

b) Batman

d) Wonder Woman

7   Who stepped into the presidency in 1945 after Franklin D. Roosevelt's sudden passing?

     a) Dwight D. Eisenhower   c) Herbert Hoover
     b) Harry S. Truman   d) Calvin Coolidge

8   What beloved 1946 holiday film gave us the warm reminder that "Every time a bell rings, an angel gets his wings"?

     a) Holiday Inn   c) It's a Wonderful Life
     b) White Christmas   d) Miracle on 34th Street

9   Which popular snack was invented in 1948 by Fritos creator Charles Elmer Doolin, quickly becoming a crunchy, cheese-flavored phenomenon?

     a) Pringles   c) Doritos
     b) Lay's Potato Chips   d) Cheetos

10　What marvelous spring toy, famous for "walking" down stairs to the tune of its catchy jingle ("...alone or in pairs, and makes a slinkety sound!"), was first demonstrated at a Philadelphia department store during Christmas 1945?

a) Lincoln Logs　　　c) Slinky

b) Tinkertoy　　　　d) LEGO

FLASHBACK FACT

Glenn Miller's recording of "Chattanooga Choo Choo" sold over a million copies, earning the very first Gold Record ever awarded in music history in February of 1942.

11　Which bebop innovator was instantly recognizable by his puffed cheeks and wild energy on stage?

a) Duke Ellington　　　c) Louis Armstrong

b) Dizzy Gillespie　　　d) Benny Goodman

12 Which 1944 film noir classic starred Barbara Stanwyck and Fred MacMurray in a tale of love and insurance fraud?

    a) White Heat   c) The Big Sleep
    b) Double Indemnity   d) Notorious

13 What product promised men "A little dab'll do ya" in its famous ads?

    a) Old Spice   c) Vitalis
    b) Brylcreem   d) Dapper Dan

14 When the men marched off to war, who was the bicep-flexing, polka-dot-bandana-wearing icon who stepped into the factories, famously declaring "We Can Do It!" as she represented millions of women joining the WWII industrial workforce?

    a) Rosie the Riveter   c) Betty Grable
    b) Wonder Woman   d) Katharine Hepburn

15 Which teenage crime-fighter joined Batman as his sidekick in 1940?

a) The Flash
b) Robin
c) Green Arrow
d) Aquaman

16 Which best-selling 1946 book shocked readers by revealing the real-life experiences of six people who survived the atomic bombing of Japan?

a) The Naked and the Dead
b) Hiroshima
c) A Bell for Adano
d) Brave New World

17 Which innovation helped families send letters overseas more quickly during World War II by photographing them onto microfilm?

a) Telegrams
b) V-Mail (Victory Mail)
c) Carrier Pigeons
d) Radio Broadcasts

18 What 1940s clothing style featured broad-shouldered jackets and knee-length skirts, reflecting the practical yet tailored look of wartime fashion?

a) Utility fashion

c) Mod

b) Flapper style

d) Glamour

19 Which big band leader had everyone swooning with "Moonlight Serenade," lifting soldiers' spirits one smooth swing at a time?

a) Bing Crosby

c) Glenn Miller

b) Louis Armstrong

d) Tommy Dorsey

20 What international organization was formed in 1945 to promote peace and cooperation among countries?

a) United Nations

c) European Union

b) NATO

d) World Bank

FLASHBACK FACT

V-Mail (short for Victory Mail) was a clever system during World War II where letters were photographed onto microfilm, shipped overseas in tiny rolls, and then printed back onto paper near their destination. This saved tons of cargo space and meant soldiers could get news from home much faster.

21 Which silent-era legend broke his silence in 1940, starring in The Great Dictator and delivering a speech that gave audiences chills?

a) Jack Oakie
b) Charlie Chaplin

c) Dean Martin
d) Harold Lloyd

22 Who stole hearts around the world in 1946, singing of life through rose-colored glasses with "La Vie en Rose"?

a) Josephine Baker
b) Edith Piaf

c) Lucienne Delyle
d) Damia

23 Which 1940s kitchen innovation promised to keep your Jell-O molds and casseroles fresh with its new plastic "burping" seal?

a) Rubbermaid

b) Tupperware

c) Pyrex

d) Ziploc

24 What catchy Broadway tune from 1943 had everyone singing, "Oh, what a beautiful mornin'"?

a) Carousel

b) Oklahoma!

c) Brigadoon

d) South Pacific

25 Which company introduced instant photography in 1948, letting families watch their photos develop before their eyes?

a) Polaroid

b) Kodak

c) Sony

d) Fuji

26 Which 1948 music innovation let listeners enjoy full albums without flipping the record every few minutes?

a) 78 RPM Record   c) 45 RPM Record
b) 33 1/3 RPM LP Record   d) Reel-to-reel tape

27 Which cigarette brand dominated 1940s radio and stamped the initials "LSMFT" on every pack?

a) Marlboro   c) Camel
b) Lucky Strike   d) Old Gold

28 Which 1949 Broadway hit swept audiences away with the romantic ballad "Some Enchanted Evening"?

a) South Pacific   c) Carousel
b) Singin' in the Rain   d) Brigadoon

29 In 1947, which player broke Major League Baseball's color barrier when he debuted with the Brooklyn Dodgers?

a) Jackie Robinson

b) Joe DiMaggio

c) Satchel Paige

d) Hank Greenberg

30 Which TV network made history in 1948 by launching Douglas Edwards and the News, America's first nightly newscast?

a) CBS

b) FOX

c) PBS

d) WB

FLASHBACK FACT

Lucky Strike was everywhere in the 1940s, from sponsoring Your Hit Parade on radio to being tucked into soldiers' rations. The "LSMFT" slogan ("Lucky Strike Means Fine Tobacco") was so common that kids joked it meant "Loose Straps Mean Falling Trousers" (among other variations).

Cruisin' Through the Rockin' '50s

The 1950s were a decade of milkshakes, jukeboxes, and brand-new rock 'n' roll. Families laughed together watching I Love Lucy and The Honeymooners, kids practiced their hula hoop tricks in the yard, and teenagers crowded into diners for burgers, fries, and a song from Elvis. Drive-in movies lit up the summer nights, cars rolled out with shiny fins, and baseball heroes became household names. It was a time of saddle shoes, sock hops, and plenty of fun. Slip on your dancing shoes, turn up the music, and let's see how well you remember the '50s!

31 What classic 1950s sitcom featured the famous chocolate factory scene, where two friends struggled to keep up with a conveyor belt of candies?

a) Father Knows Best c) I Love Lucy
b) The Honeymooners d) Leave It to Beaver

32 Which singer became known as the "King of Rock 'n' Roll" after hits like Hound Dog and Jailhouse Rock?

a) Chuck Berry c) Elvis Presley
b) Buddy Holly d) Little Richard

33 Which 1958 Wham-O toy craze had millions of kids twirling colorful plastic around their waists?

a) Skip-It c) Yo-Yo
b) Hula Hoop d) Jump Rope

34 Which Yankees pitcher made baseball history in 1956 by tossing the only perfect game ever in the World Series?

a) Bob Gibson
b) Sandy Koufax
c) Don Larsen
d) Whitey Ford

35 Which sugar-free beverage, introduced in 1952, was marketed to diabetics before diet sodas became mainstream?

a) Coca-Cola
b) Pepsi
c) No-Cal
d) RC Cola

36 What was the name of the first artificial satellite, launched by the Soviet Union in 1957?

a) Explorer 1
b) Sputnik 1
c) Luna 2
d) Vanguard

37 Which car company introduced the stylish Thunderbird in 1955, sparking a craze for sporty two-seaters?

a) Chevrolet   c) Chrysler
b) Ford   d) Buick

38 What 1955 Disney film introduced kids to a spaghetti-sharing pup named Tramp?

a) 101 Dalmatians   c) Bambi
b) Lady and the Tramp d) Cinderella

39 Which fast-food chain opened its first restaurant in Des Plaines, Illinois, in 1955?

a) Burger King   c) McDonald's
b) Wendy's   d) Dairy Queen

40 Which organ made medical history in 1954 as the first to be successfully transplanted, thanks to a groundbreaking surgery between identical twins?

a) Heart   c) Lung
b) Kidney   d) Liver

FLASHBACK FACT

Elvis didn't just wiggle on stage, he practically stopped the nation. His 1956 performance on The Ed Sullivan Show drew 60 million viewers, more than half of all TVs in America at the time!

41 Which 1950s teen idol became a symbol of youthful rebellion in Rebel Without a Cause, only to die tragically in a car crash at 24?

a) Marlon Brando   c) James Dean
b) Elvis Presley   d) Paul Newman

42 Who became a household name as the host of American Bandstand, the show that had teens dancing in living rooms across America?

    a) Ed Sullivan   c) Dick Clark
    b) Alan Freed   d) Lawrence Welk

43 Which New York Yankee great retired in 1951, then made even bigger headlines in 1954 when he married Marilyn Monroe?

    a) Joe DiMaggio   c) Yogi Berra
    b) Jackie Robinson   d) Duke Snider

44 Which 1955 film featured Bill Haley's "Rock Around the Clock" in its opening credits, helping launch rock 'n' roll into the mainstream?

    a) Blackboard Jungle   c) Jailhouse Rock
    b) Rebel Without a   d) Let's Rock!
    Cause

45 Which Hollywood starlet swapped the silver screen for a tiara when she married Prince Rainier of Monaco in 1956?

a) Grace Kelly   c) Elizabeth Taylor
b) Audrey Hepburn   d) Debbie Reynolds

46 Which 1950s toy became the first ever advertised on television, hitting screens in 1952?

a) View-Master   c) Etch A Sketch
b) Mr. Potato Head   d) Barbie

47 Which New York Giants center fielder made history in 1954 with "The Catch," sprinting deep into center field for an over-the-shoulder grab that left fans speechless?

a) Jackie Robinson   c) Willie Mays
b) Hank Aaron   d) Roy Campanella

48 Which suburban innovation opened in 1956 in Edina, Minnesota, becoming the first fully enclosed, climate-controlled shopping mall in the U.S.?

    a) Mall of America   c) Galleria
    b) Southdale Center   d) King of Prussia Mall

49 Who played Marilyn Monroe's sharp-tongued best friend in Gentlemen Prefer Blondes (1953)?

    a) Jane Russell   c) Shirley MacLaine
    b) Judy Garland   d) Doris Day

50 Which 1950s Broadway smash, featuring classics like "Shall We Dance?" and "Getting to Know You," swept audiences off their feet with its royal setting and unforgettable score?

    a) Oklahoma!   c) Carousel
    b) The King and I   d) My Fair Lady

51 Which 1950s comedy-quiz show was guaranteed to deliver laughs with Groucho Marx's razor-sharp wit and unscripted contestant interviews—all before the announcer shouted, "Say the secret word!" and a ridiculous toy duck descended with a cash prize of a crisp $100 bill?

a) Beat the Clock

b) You Bet Your Life

c) The $64,000 Question

d) What's My Line?

52 Which comedy duo turned a simple payphone call to "Alexander 4444" into a fan-favorite gag on their early-1950s TV show?

a) The Marx Brothers

b) Abbott and Costello

c) Laurel and Hardy

d) The Three Stooges

FLASHBACK FACT

During World War II, Abbott & Costello performed for U.S. troops so often that the War Department credited them with raising millions in morale and bond sales. Their comedy tours were considered just as vital to the home front as swing bands and Hollywood films.

53 Which soda brand ran the jingle, "Be sociable, have a...", starting in the 1950s?

a) Pepsi
b) Coca-Cola

c) Dr Pepper
d) 7-Up

54 Which children's TV show, debuting in 1955, featured a giant mouse and launched the careers of stars like Annette Funicello?

a) The Mickey Mouse Club
b) Romper Room

c) Howdy Doody
d) Captain Kangaroo

55 Which "Peanuts" character first appeared in Charles Schulz's comic strip in 1950?

a) Charlie Brown
b) Snoopy

c) Lucy
d) Linus

56 The Edsel, launched by Ford in 1957, became a legendary flop, costing the company an estimated $250 million (over $2.5 billion today). What was the most distinctive (and widely mocked) feature of its highly publicized design?

a) The rotating, propeller-like hubcaps that were easily lost

b) The vertical grille that many critics compared to a toilet seat or a horse collar

c) A push-button transmission located in the center of the steering wheel hub

d) Headlights mounted on the top of the front fenders like insect eyes

57 Which late 1950s quiz show became notorious when producers were caught feeding contestants answers, leading to one of TV's biggest scandals?

a) Twenty-One

b) The $64,000 Question

c) Tic-Tac-Dough

d) What's My Line?

58 Which scientific breakthrough was first described in 1953, when researchers published a model that forever changed our understanding of genetics?

a) The development of insulin

b) The structure of DNA

c) The creation of the polio vaccine

d) The discovery of penicillin

59 Which theme park first opened its gates in 1955, welcoming guests to "the happiest place on earth" with Main Street, Fantasyland, and a dream?

a) Disney World

b) Disneyland

c) Magic Kingdom

d) EPCOT

60 Which 1950s fashion trend had teen girls twirling on the dance floor in wide skirts puffed up with layers of crinoline?

a) Poodle skirts

b) Mini skirts

c) Pencil skirts

d) Bell bottoms

61 Which 1959 board game turned kitchen tables into battlefields, challenging players to deploy armies and conquer the world?

a) Sorry!

b) Battleship

c) Candy Land

d) Risk

FLASHBACK FACT

Disneyland's 1955 opening was so chaotic that the asphalt melted in the summer heat, women's high heels sank into Main Street, and some guests even climbed fences to sneak inside. It was messy, magical, and unforgettable.

62 Which lemon-lime soda called itself "The All-Family Drink" in 1950s ads, showing cheerful families sipping together around the dinner table?

a) Sprite

b) 7-Up

c) RC Cola

d) Tab

63 Which blonde bombshell stole the show as Sugar "Kane" in the 1959 comedy classic Some Like It Hot?

a) Jayne Mansfield

c) Debbie Reynolds

b) Marilyn Monroe

d) Grace Kelly

64 Which 1950s teen hairstyle, made famous by Elvis and the "greaser" look, was styled high in the front with slicked-back sides?

a) The flat top

c) The crew cut

b) The pompadour

d) The shag

65 Which Looney Tunes character popped through a drum at the end of cartoons to stutter out "Th-th-th-that's all, folks!"?

a) Mickey Mouse

c) Bugs Bunny

b) Porky Pig

d) Daffy Duck

66 Which 1950s Yankee superstar, known as the "Commerce Comet," thrilled fans with his power hitting and all-American charm?

a) Mickey Mantle
b) Willie Mays
c) Hank Aaron
d) Roger Maris

67 Which snack cake, first introduced decades earlier, became a 1950s lunchbox favorite thanks to its new signature squiggly-topped cream filling?

a) Hostess Twinkies
b) Ding Dongs
c) Hostess CupCakes
d) Little Debbie Oatmeal Pies

68 Which 1950s plastic toy turned backyards into splash zones, as kids ditched their cowboy cap guns for watery showdowns?

a) Super Soaker
b) Cap gun
c) Squirt gun
d) Nerf Blaster

69 Which 1950 toy came in a little plastic egg and amazed kids by stretching, bouncing, and even picking up newspaper ink?

a) Play-Doh   c) Slinky
b) Silly Putty   d) Yo-Yo

70 Which 1950s rock 'n' roll legend strummed out the 1957 hit "Peggy Sue," named after his drummer's girlfriend?

a) Buddy Holly   c) Little Richard
b) Chuck Berry   d) Jerry Lee Lewis

71 Which fashion item, made famous by Marlon Brando in The Wild One (1953), caused such a teen craze that some schools banned it for "encouraging juvenile delinquency"?

a) Leather jacket   c) Denim overalls
b) Fedora hat   d) White gloves

FLASHBACK FACT

In the 1950s, a burger cost about 15¢ and a malt around 25¢ - the perfect price for a teenager's weekly allowance. On Friday nights, spare change meant cruising to the drive-in, jukeboxes blaring, and carhops on skates delivering trays of burgers and shakes.

72 Which toy company introduced a glamorous new doll in 1959, complete with a striped swimsuit, high heels, and a name that would become iconic?

a) Hasbro

b) Mattel

c) Fisher-Price

d) Ideal

73 Which 1959 TV series followed Eliot Ness and his fearless team as they took on Chicago's most notorious gangsters, with Robert Stack leading the charge?

a) Perry Mason

b) Dragnet

c) The Untouchables

d) Alfred Hitchcock Presents

74 Which smooth-voiced 1950s crooner had fans swooning with hits like "Catch a Falling Star" and "Magic Moments"?

a) Frank Sinatra

b) Bing Crosby

c) Perry Como

d) Dean Martin

75 Which 1950s luxury car turned heads with its dramatic chrome and tailfins that stretched nearly four feet into the air, making it a symbol of automotive excess?

a) Chevrolet Corvette

b) Cadillac Eldorado

c) Ford Thunderbird

d) Chrysler Imperial

76 Which early 1950s preschool TV show, hosted by "Miss Frances," rang a little bell to welcome kids and taught them manners, crafts, and basic skills?

a) Romper Room

b) Captain Kangaroo

c) Howdy Doody

d) Ding Dong School

77 Which candy, created for WWII soldiers so chocolate wouldn't melt in their pockets, charmed 1950s snackers with the slogan "melts in your mouth, not in your hand"?

a) Skittles

b) M&Ms

c) Reese's Pieces

d) Milk Duds

78 Which 1950 comic strip introduced readers to a lazy Army private and his misfit crew at Camp Swampy, becoming a newspaper favorite for decades?

a) Beetle Bailey

b) Peanuts

c) Dennis the Menace

d) Richie Rich

79 Who took on the role of Moses in Cecil B. DeMille's 1956 biblical epic The Ten Commandments, booming "Let my people go!" in one of cinema's most iconic performances?

a) Kirk Douglas

b) Gregory Peck

c) Charlton Heston

d) Yul Brynner

80 Which Major League Baseball team broke Brooklyn's heart in 1958 by packing up and heading west to Los Angeles?

a) Dodgers
b) Yankees
c) Giants
d) Cubs

81 Which American scientist became a national hero in 1955 when he announced the first successful polio vaccine, bringing hope to millions of families?

a) Albert Sabin
b) Jonas Salk
c) Linus Pauling
d) Edward Jenner

FLASHBACK FACT

When Barbie debuted at the 1959 New York Toy Fair for just $3, she caused a sensation. More than 300,000 dolls flew off shelves that first year, kicking off a fashion doll revolution.

82 Which classic snack, sold at ball games and theaters, promised "candy-coated popcorn, peanuts, and a prize" in its famous jingle?

    a) Raisinets   c) Goobers
    b) Cracker Jack   d) M&M's Peanut

83 Who was the host of This Is Your Life, the long-running TV show that surprised guests with stories from their past?

    a) Ralph Edwards   c) Groucho Marx
    b) Ed Sullivan   d) Jack Paar

84 Which fast-food chain, franchised by Colonel Sanders beginning in 1952, spread his famous recipe of "11 herbs and spices" across the country as he drove from diner to diner with a pressure cooker in his trunk?

    a) KFC   c) Church's Chicken
    b) Popeyes   d) Bojangles

85 Which accordion-loving bandleader filled living rooms with "champagne music" when his variety show hit national TV in 1955?

   a) Guy Lombardo   c) Lawrence Welk
   b) Glenn Miller   d) Benny Goodman

86 Which heavyweight legend, nicknamed "The Brockton Blockbuster," retired in 1956 with a perfect 49–0 record?

   a) Joe Louis   c) Floyd Patterson
   b) Rocky Marciano   d) Sonny Liston

87 Which 1951 toy let kids stick reusable vinyl outfits onto glossy boards, dressing up characters again and again with no glue required?

   a) Lite-Brite   c) View-Master
   b) Colorforms   d) Spirograph

88 Which 1951 comic strip introduced readers to a mischievous blond troublemaker and his loyal dog Ruff, quickly becoming a newspaper favorite?

    a) Dennis the Menace   c) Peanuts
    b) Calvin and Hobbes   d) Family Circus

89 In 1957, which tennis champ made history as the first African American to win Wimbledon and celebrated with a ticker-tape parade down the streets of New York?

    a) Althea Gibson   c) Zina Garrison
    b) Arthur Ashe   d) Billie Jean King

90 Which iconic baking brand popularized boxed cake mixes in the 1950s by encouraging home bakers to add their own fresh eggs, making the treats feel more "homemade"?

    a) Jell-O   c) Betty Crocker
    b) Duncan Hines   d) Hostess

91 Which 1957 Broadway smash marched into history with the brassy showstopper "Seventy-Six Trombones," later becoming a hit film?

a) The Music Man

b) Guys and Dolls

c) My Fair Lady

d) West Side Story

FLASHBACK FACT

When Mr. Potato Head came out, he didn't come with a plastic potato. Kids were expected to use a real potato from the kitchen and stick the plastic face parts into it! It wasn't until 1964 that Hasbro added the plastic potato body we know today.

92 Which 1950s grocery staple claimed to "build strong bodies 12 ways," thanks to a splashy ad campaign about added vitamins and minerals?

a) Pepsi

b) Milk

c) Coca-Cola

d) Wonder Bread

93 Which TV dog trotted onto screens in 1954, rescuing kids and stealing hearts, and went on to become a household name for decades?

a) Benji
b) Lassie
c) Rin Tin Tin
d) Old Yeller

94 What classic candy, first sold in 1907, became a post-war favorite again in the 1950s thanks to its shiny silver wrappers?

a) Reese's Cups
b) Hershey's Kisses
c) Milk Duds
d) Snickers

95 Which 1958 kitchen innovation promised busy cooks they could take their dish from freezer to oven to table, all in the same pretty blue-cornflower pan?

a) Corning Ware
b) Pyrex
c) Farberware
d) Revere Ware

96   Which suave, spooky actor became a household name in the 1950s thanks to his chilling roles in horror films like House of Wax (1953)?

   a) Bela Lugosi   c) Vincent Price
   b) Boris Karloff   d) Lon Chaney Jr.

97   Which 1954 monster movie terrified audiences with a gill-man who rose from the depths to terrorize scientists on an Amazon expedition?

   a) Godzilla   c) King Kong
   b) The Creature from   d) Them!
   the Black Lagoon

98   Which fashion accessory became a must-have teen status symbol in the 1950s, often sewn onto jackets to show school pride?

   a) Varsity letters   c) Bow ties
   b) Neckerchiefs   d) Pocket watches

99 Which smooth-voiced 1950s crooner turned "Mona Lisa" into a hit and made TV history as the first African American to host a national variety show?

    a) Nat King Cole   c) Dean Martin
    b) Frank Sinatra   d) Bing Crosby

100 Which 1953 frozen dinner innovation, sold in shiny aluminum trays, was marketed as the perfect way to enjoy a meal in front of the TV?

    a) Swanson TV Dinners   c) Banquet Meals
    b) Hungry-Man   d) Lean Cuisine

101 Which teen magazine, launched in 1957, plastered Elvis, James Dean, and other dreamy idols on its covers, setting the stage for the teen fan craze?

    a) Seventeen   c) Tiger Beat
    b) Teen Beat   d) 16 Magazine

FLASHBACK FACT

Swanson invented TV dinners in 1953 thanks to a massive surplus of leftover Thanksgiving turkey. Their brilliant last-minute solution? Pack the turkey and sides into aluminum trays, freeze them, and market them as "TV dinners" - perfectly timed for America's new obsession with eating in front of the television.

102 Which 1959 Hollywood epic galloped into history with a legendary chariot race and a then-record 11 Oscar wins?

a) Around the World in 80 Days

b) On the Waterfront

c) Ben-Hur

d) The Bridge on the River Kwai

103 In 1955, who made history by refusing to give up her seat on a Montgomery bus, sparking a 381-day boycott that changed the nation?

a) Daisy Bates

b) Rosa Parks

c) Ella Baker

d) Coretta Scott King

104 Which legendary filmmaker brought his dry wit and a spooky silhouette to TV in 1955, hosting an anthology series that became a classic of suspense?

a) Orson Welles
b) Alfred Hitchcock

c) Rod Serling
d) Jackie Gleason

105 In response to the launch of Sputnik, which U.S. agency was created in 1958 to take the lead in space exploration?

a) NOAA
b) FAA

c) NASA
d) DARPA

106 Which two states were admitted to the Union in 1959 as the 49th and 50th states?

a) Alaska & Arizona
b) Alaska & Hawaii
c) New Mexico &

Alaska
d) Hawaii & Puerto
Rico

107 Which soft, colorful compound started as wallpaper cleaner but became a beloved kids' toy in 1956, especially after getting a boost from Captain Kangaroo?

a) Silly Putty

b) Etch A Sketch

c) Play-Doh

d) Tinkertoy

108 Which 1950s superstar caused a media frenzy when he traded his blue suede shoes for Army boots after being drafted in 1958?

a) Buddy Holly

b) Frank Sinatra

c) Johnny Cash

d) Elvis Presley

109 Which 1956 law, championed by President Eisenhower, paved the way (literally!) for America's massive Interstate Highway System?

a) Highway Beautification Act

b) National Traffic and Motor Vehicle Safety Act

c) Federal-Aid Highway Act

d) Public Roads Modernization Act

110 Originally called the "Pluto Platter," which flying disc was renamed after a pie company's tins that college kids tossed for fun and became a Wham-O sensation in 1957?

a) Aerobie
b) Frisbee
c) Boomerang
d) Hula Disc

111 Which 1959 tragedy, later immortalized in the song "American Pie," is often called "The Day the Music Died"?

a) The payola scandal hearings
b) A plane crash that killed Buddy Holly, Ritchie Valens, and J.P. "The Big Bopper" Richardson
c) A riot at a rock 'n' roll concert
d) The shutdown of a major record label

FLASHBACK FACT

By the end of the 1950s, nearly 90% of American households owned a television, up from less than 10% at the decade's start. In just ten years, TV went from a novelty to the nation's favorite pastime, forever changing family nights in the living room.

112 Which popular credit card, launched in 1950, let New Yorkers pay at dozens of restaurants with a single card?

a) Visa
b) Diners Club
c) American Express
d) Mastercard

113 Which invention became a must-have household appliance in the 1950s, changing the way families tackled laundry day?

a) Electric iron
b) Clothes dryer
c) Fabric softener
d) Spin mop

114 Which 1950s novelty toy let wannabe secret agents write invisible messages that could only be revealed with heat or a special light?

a) Spy Pen
b) Magic Marker
c) Decoder Ring
d) Silly Putty

115 Which planned suburban community, built on Long Island after WWII, became a symbol of the 1950s housing boom?

a) Levittown   c) Massapequa
b) Greenbelt   d) Rockville Centre

116 Which Peanuts character, first seen clutching his famous blue blanket in the 1950s, introduced the world to the idea of a "security blanket"?

a) Charlie Brown   c) Schroeder
b) Linus   d) Pigpen

117 Which 1950s toy let kids use a magnetic wand to give a bald cartoon face wild new hairstyles, beards, and brows again and again?

a) Mr. Potato Head   c) Etch A Sketch
b) Wooly Willy   d) Colorforms

118 In which 1950s film does Audrey Hepburn play a runaway princess who explores the city on a Vespa with Gregory Peck?

a) Sabrina
b) Roman Holiday
c) Funny Face
d) Breakfast at Tiffany's

119 Which classic candy, often found in foil rolls in lunchboxes and glove compartments, was famously advertised in the 1950s as "the candy with the hole"?

a) Life Savers
b) Necco Wafers
c) Milk Duds
d) Smarties

120 Which 1950s game challenged players to remove thin sticks from a pile without disturbing the others?

a) Jenga
b) Pick-Up Sticks
c) Barrel of Monkeys
d) Mousetrap

121 Which 1950s hairstyle had women sleeping in bobby pins and rollers overnight to wake up with perfect tight curls?

a) The beehive   c) The pin curl
b) The pageboy   d) The bouffant

FLASHBACK FACT

Wooly Willy was one of the cheapest toys of the 1950s, selling for just 29¢. With a magnetic wand and iron filings, kids gave Willy wild hairdos, mustaches, and eyebrows. It was simple, silly, and endlessly entertaining.

122 Which children's classic by Dr. Seuss, published in 1957, told the story of a grumpy green character who preferred to spend time alone with his dog?

a) The Cat in the Hat   Christmas
b) Charlotte's Web   d) Harold and the
c) How the Grinch Stole   Purple Crayon

123 Which 1950s film featured Marlon Brando in a leather jacket saying, "What are you rebelling against?"

    a) On the Waterfront   c) A Streetcar Named
    b) The Wild One   Desire
                            d) East of Eden

124 In The Honeymooners, what was Ralph Kramden's job?

    a) Milkman   c) Sewer worker
    b) Bus driver   d) Newspaper delivery
                            man

125 Which 1950s singer, known for his silky ballads like "Chances Are," became the soundtrack to countless sock hops and slow dances?

    a) Nat King Cole   c) Tony Bennett
    b) Johnny Mathis   d) Frank Sinatra

126 Which black-and-white shoes were all the rage with 1950s teens, especially when paired with bobby socks at a sock hop?

a) Penny loafers   c) Converse
b) Saddle shoes   d) Mary Janes

127 Which 1950s comic book sweetheart, the ultimate girl-next-door, had a long-running crush on redheaded Archie Andrews?

a) Veronica Lodge   c) Josie
b) Betty Cooper   d) Cheryl Blossom

128 In which 1955 film do Grace Kelly and Cary Grant trade witty banter and chase jewels along the glamorous French Riviera?

a) Rear Window   c) High Society
b) To Catch a Thief   d) Dial M for Murder

129 Which candy, a movie-theater favorite in the 1950s, combined chewy caramel with a chocolatey coating?

a) Milk Duds

b) Tootsie Rolls

c) Bit-O-Honey

d) Sugar Babies

130 Which wildly popular 1950s kids' show featured a freckle-faced marionette, a lively studio "peanut gallery," and a host named Buffalo Bob?

a) Romper Room

b) The Howdy Doody Show

c) Captain Kangaroo

d) Ding Dong School

131 Which line of miniature die-cast toy cars, first sold in 1953, became a worldwide craze with kids collecting pocket-sized vehicles?

a) Matchbox

b) Hot Wheels

c) Silly Putty

d) Wheel Lovers

FLASHBACK FACT

Matchbox cars were named after the tiny boxes they came in, just like real matchboxes! The clever packaging turned "Matchbox" into the go-to name for toy cars around the world.

132 Which 1954 musical paired Bing Crosby and Danny Kaye for a snow-dusted, song-filled holiday classic featuring the unforgettable title tune?

a) Holiday Inn

b) White Christmas

c) Going My Way

d) High Society

133 Which 1956 TV gadget let viewers change channels without getting off the couch by using ultrasonic "clicks"?

a) Zenith Space Command

b) Magnavox AutoTune

c) Philco TeleGuide

d) RCA ColorTrak Remote

134 Which 1950s singer had teens "tweet-tweet-tweeting" along to his 1958 hit "Rockin' Robin"?

a) Bobby Day
b) Frankie Avalon
c) Ricky Nelson
d) Pat Boone

135 Which mid-century kitchen staple promised to tackle even the toughest baked-on grease, saving homemakers from endless scrubbing?

a) Windex
b) Easy-Off Oven Cleaner
c) Lysol
d) Pine-Sol

136 Which 1950s movie monster emerged from the depths after atomic testing, stomped through Tokyo, and became a cinematic legend?

a) The Blob
b) Godzilla
c) The Creature from the Black Lagoon
d) Them!

137 Which TV western, debuting in 1959, followed the Cartwright family on the Ponderosa Ranch?

a) Bonanza
b) My Favorite Martian
c) Gunsmoke
d) Rawhide

138 Which candy, a 1950s favorite, came in a wax-paper roll filled with pastel discs that crunched with that unmistakable chalky sweetness?

a) Smarties
b) Necco Wafers
c) Sweetarts
d) Life Savers

139 Which 1950s film starred Tony Curtis and Burt Lancaster in a gritty tale of New York journalism?

a) Sweet Smell of Success
b) Some Like It Hot
c) The Defiant Ones
d) Spartacus

140 Which candy, a movie-theater favorite in the 1950s, combined chewy caramel with a chocolatey coating?

a) Milk Duds

b) Tootsie Rolls

c) Bit-O-Honey

d) Sugar Babies

FLASHBACK FACT

The 1956 Zenith Space Command changed channels with ultrasonic "clicks" made by tiny hammers – no batteries needed. That's where "clicker" comes from!

Peace, Love, and the '60s

The 1960s were groovy, colorful, and unforgettable. The Beatles crossed the ocean to change music forever, Motown lit up the airwaves, and Woodstock turned a muddy field into history. TVs brought us The Flintstones, Star Trek, and the first steps on the moon. Kids traded marbles for GI Joes and Barbie's new Dreamhouse, while teenagers cruised around in Mustangs and VW buses. Miniskirts, go-go boots, and tie-dye ruled the closets, and breakfast was easier with Pop-Tarts and Tang. It was a decade of change, laughter, and incredible pop culture, so grab your bell bottoms, spin a Beatles record, and see how much you remember about the swinging '60s!

141 Which psychedelic guitar hero famously set his instrument ablaze during a mind-blowing performance at the 1967 Monterey Pop Festival?

a) Eric Clapton
b) Pete Townshend
c) Jimi Hendrix
d) Carlos Santana

142 Which late 1960s Disney film featured a Volkswagen Beetle with a mind of its own?

a) The Absent-Minded Professor
b) The Love Bug
c) That Darn Cat!
d) The Computer Wore Tennis Shoes

143 Which 1964 breakfast cereal made mornings more fun with colorful marshmallows and the slogan "They're magically delicious"?

a) Lucky Charms
b) Cocoa Puffs
c) Froot Loops
d) Cap'n Crunch

144 Which 1965 game challenged kids to use tweezers to remove "funny bones" without touching the edges and setting off a buzzer?

a) Lite-Brite

b) Perfection

c) Operation

d) Mouse Trap

145 Which actress turned heads (and set fashion history) as the glamorous Holly Golightly in the 1961 classic Breakfast at Tiffany's?

a) Audrey Hepburn

b) Shirley MacLaine

c) Natalie Wood

d) Julie Christie

FLASHBACK FACT

The famous black dress from Breakfast at Tiffany's later sold at auction for over $900,000, making it one of the most famous film costumes ever.

146 Which car brand revved up the muscle car era in 1964 by introducing the legendary GTO?

a) Ford

b) Pontiac

c) Chevrolet

d) Dodge

147 Which 1963 children's book introduced readers to Max, who traveled to an island of mischievous creatures?

a) The Snowy Day

b) Where the Wild Things Are

c) Green Eggs and Ham

d) Make Way for Ducklings

148 Which 1964 stop-motion Christmas special featured Burl Ives as the snowman narrator and the song "A Holly Jolly Christmas"?

a) Rudolph the Red-Nosed Reindeer

b) Frosty the Snowman

c) Santa Claus Is Comin' to Town

d) The Little Drummer Boy

149 Which 1967 film featured Warren Beatty and Faye Dunaway as Depression-era bank robbers?

a) The Wild Bunch
b) Bonnie and Clyde
c) Gun Crazy
d) The Front Page

150 Which 1969 festival turned a New York farm into a sea of music, mud, and nearly half a million peace-loving fans?

a) Woodstock
b) Monterey Pop
c) Isle of Wight
d) Altamont

151 Which 1963 toy let kids whip up real mini cakes and cookies using the power of a single light bulb?

a) Creepy Crawlers
b) Suzy Homemaker Oven
c) Barbie Dream Kitchen
d) Easy-Bake Oven

152 Which 1962 spy thriller introduced Sean Connery as 007, kicking off the James Bond movie phenomenon?

a) Goldfinger
b) From Russia with Love

c) Dr. No
d) Thunderball

153 Which 1966 TV show featured Adam West as the caped crusader, complete with "POW!" and "BAM!" fight scenes?

a) Superman
b) Batman

c) Green Hornet
d) The Flash

154 Which 1964 breakfast treat came in shiny foil wrappers and caused such a craze that it sold out in just two weeks?

a) Toaster Strudel
b) Pop-Tarts

c) Nutri-Grain Bars
d) Breakfast Bars

155 Which 1969 space mission made history when Neil Armstrong took "one giant leap for mankind"?

a) Apollo 10

b) Apollo 11

c) Gemini 12

d) Mercury 9

FLASHBACK FACT

In 1969, Buzz Aldrin reported seeing a mysterious object during the famous space mission. NASA explained it as a reflective panel from the rocket, but the sighting has fueled UFO debates ever since.

156 Which Motown girl group had hits like "Stop! In the Name of Love" and "Baby Love"?

a) The Ronettes

b) The Supremes

c) The Shirelles

d) Martha & the Vandellas

157 Which 1963 cereal invited kids to "follow their nose!" with Toucan Sam leading the way to fruity, colorful breakfasts?

a) Cocoa Puffs
b) Froot Loops
c) Lucky Charms
d) Apple Jacks

158 Which futuristic cartoon family zipped around in flying cars and had a robot maid named Rosie?

a) The Jetsons
b) The Flintstones
c) Lost in Space
d) Fantastic Four

159 Which 1965 musical sent Julie Andrews twirling through the Alps and into movie history alongside Christopher Plummer?

a) My Fair Lady
b) The Sound of Music
c) Doctor Zhivago
d) Mary Poppins

FLASHBACK FACT

Julie Andrews nearly turned down The Sound of Music because she worried it would be "too sugary" after Mary Poppins. Luckily, she said yes and the movie became a timeless classic.

160 Which 1964 toy line marched onto store shelves with poseable "action figures," letting kids play soldier in style?

a) Green Army Men
b) Major Matt Mason
c) G.I. Joe
d) Johnny West

161 Which 1967 counterculture event in San Francisco became known as the "Summer of Love"?

a) Golden Gate Festival
b) Monterey Pop Festival
c) Haight-Ashbury gatherings
d) Altamont

162 Which British teen with a pixie cut and iconic lashes became known as "The Face of the '60s"?

a) Jean Shrimpton

b) Twiggy

c) Penelope Tree

d) Veruschka

163 Which 1968 sci-fi masterpiece invited moviegoers on "the ultimate trip" with mind-bending visuals and a mysterious black monolith?

a) Planet of the Apes

b) 2001: A Space Odyssey

c) Barbarella

d) Fantastic Voyage

164 Which folk trio had hits with "Puff, the Magic Dragon" and "Lemon Tree"?

a) The Kingston Trio

b) Peter, Paul and Mary

c) The Chad Mitchell Trio

d) The New Christy Minstrels

165 Which 1965 sitcom starred Barbara Eden as a mischievous magical woman who causes trouble for an unsuspecting astronaut?

a) Bewitched

b) I Dream of Jeannie

c) That Girl

d) The Flying Nun

FLASHBACK FACT

Barbara Eden's costume was considered so risqué for TV that network censors insisted her belly button remain covered!

166 Which 1961 Disney animated film featured 101 spotted puppies and a villain named Cruella De Vil?

a) Lady and the Tramp

b) 101 Dalmatians

c) The Aristocats

d) The Jungle Book

167 Which American boxer, then known as Cassius Clay, won a gold medal at the 1960 Rome Olympics?

a) Joe Frazier
b) Sonny Liston

c) Muhammad Ali
d) George Foreman

168 Which now-iconic snack started as a clever way to use leftover tortillas at Disneyland, leading to its national launch in 1966?

a) Pringles
b) Bugles

c) Doritos
d) Cheetos

169 Which 1960s sitcom's "star" was a palomino who delivered punchlines to his owner, but stayed silent for everyone else?

a) Mister Ed
b) Green Acres

c) My Favorite Martian
d) Petticoat Junction

170 Which iconic American car set a record in 1965 as the best-selling single model ever, with over 1 million sold?

a) Ford Mustang

c) Dodge Charger

b) Chevrolet Impala

d) Pontiac GTO

FLASHBACK FACT

In 1965, the Chevrolet Impala cruised into the record books by selling 1,074,925 cars in a single model year, a jaw-dropping feat no other American car has matched since. It became the best-selling car of the year and still holds the title for the highest single-year sales of any U.S. model.

171 Which 1966 TV show introduced Captain Kirk, Spock, and the starship Enterprise?

a) Lost in Space

c) Voyage to the

b) Star Trek

Bottom of the Sea

d) Thunderbirds

172 Which comedian became famous for playing the good-natured Gomer Pyle, a gas station attendant turned Marine?

a) Don Knotts
b) Jim Nabors
c) Andy Griffith
d) Jerry Lewis

173 Which 1968 thriller starred Mia Farrow as a young woman who feared her neighbors were part of a satanic cult?

a) The Exorcist
b) Rosemary's Baby
c) The Omen
d) Don't Look Now

174 Which soft drink adopted the slogan "Things go better with..." in 1963?

a) Pepsi
b) Coca-Cola
c) 7-Up
d) Dr Pepper

175 Which 1967 detective drama starred Sidney Poitier as a Philadelphia cop investigating a murder in the South?

a) A Patch of Blue
b) In the Heat of the Night

c) Guess Who's Coming to Dinner
d) To Sir, with Love

176 Which 1960s toy used plastic gears and colorful pens to make hypnotic swirling designs that felt like pure magic?

a) Lite-Brite
b) Spirograph

c) Etch A Sketch
d) Magic 8-Ball

177 Which 1968 film featured Steve McQueen in a thrilling car chase through San Francisco?

a) The Great Escape
b) Bullitt

c) The Thomas Crown Affair
d) Le Mans

178 Which 1960s sitcom whistled its way into TV history, signaling its easygoing charm from the very first notes of its iconic opening theme?

a) Green Acres
b) The Andy Griffith Show

c) Petticoat Junction
d) The Beverly Hillbillies

179 Which NASA astronaut became the first American to orbit Earth in 1962?

a) Gus Grissom
b) Alan Shepard

c) John Glenn
d) Michael Collins

180 Which late-1960s Broadway rock musical brought the counterculture to the stage with songs like "Aquarius" and "Let the Sunshine In"?

a) Godspell
b) Hair

c) Company
d) Jesus Christ Superstar

181 Which 1963 Alfred Hitchcock thriller starring Tippi Hedren was based on a 1952 short story by Daphne du Maurier?

a) Torn Curtain   c) Marnie
b) The Birds   d) Topaz

182 Which 1969 Saturday-morning cartoon followed a gang of teen sleuths and their talking Great Dane as they cruised around in the Mystery Machine?

a) The Archies   c) Josie and the
b) Scooby-Doo, Where   Pussycats
Are You!   d) Speed Buggy

183 Which British band's 1969 second album included the song 'Whole Lotta Love'?

a) Led Zeppelin   c) The Doors
b) The Rolling Stones   d) The Who

FLASHBACK FACT

The name "Led Zeppelin" came from a joke by The Who's Keith Moon, who quipped the band would go over "like a lead balloon." Jimmy Page swapped balloon for zeppelin and dropped the "a" in lead so no one would say "leed."

184 Which 1967 film put one couple's open-minded values to the ultimate test when their daughter introduced her new fiancé?

a) In the Heat of the Night

b) To Sir, with Love

c) Guess Who's Coming to Dinner

d) A Patch of Blue

185 What circular, chocolate-coated cake, often wrapped like a hockey puck and named after the sound of a bell, was introduced by Hostess in the late 1960s?

a) Twinkies

b) Fruit Pies

c) Ho Hos

d) Ding Dongs

186 Which children's puppet show ended its long run in 1960 after more than a decade on air?

a) Kukla, Fran and Ollie
b) The Howdy Doody Show

c) Time for Beany
d) Captain Kangaroo

187 Which U.S. president signed the Civil Rights Act of 1964 into law?

a) John F. Kennedy
b) Lyndon B. Johnson

c) Richard Nixon
d) Gerald Ford

188 Which 1969 buddy film starred Paul Newman and Robert Redford as outlaws on the run?

a) The Sting
b) Butch Cassidy and the Sundance Kid

c) The Wild Bunch
d) Easy Rider

189 Which 1960s hairstyle became a symbol of sleek, mod fashion with its precise, angular cut?

a) The Flip

b) The Sassoon

c) The Shag

d) The Farrah

190 Which classic 1960s toy let two plastic boxers duke it out in the ring until one fighter's head popped up in glorious defeat?

a) Wham-O Air Blaster

b) Rock 'Em Sock 'Em Robots

c) Mousetrap

d) Hungry Hungry Hippps

191 Which 10-year-old brainiac - who runs his own detective agency out of a garage, charges a mere 25 cents a day (plus expenses!), and first appeared in a 1963 novel - helps his police chief dad solve neighborhood cases?

a) Encyclopedia Brown

b) Henry Huggins

c) Homer Price

d) Danny Dunn

192 Which 1967 film inspired Simon & Garfunkel's hit song "Mrs. Robinson" and made Dustin Hoffman a star?

a) The Graduate
b) Midnight Cowboy
c) Cool Hand Luke
d) Bonnie and Clyde

193 Which British fashion designer is credited with creating the miniskirt?

a) Mary Quant
b) Vivienne Westwood
c) Zandra Rhodes
d) Barbara Hulanicki

194 Which 1966 Western starring Clint Eastwood became famous for its spaghetti Western style and Ennio Morricone's music?

a) A Fistful of Dollars
b) The Good, the Bad and the Ugly
c) For a Few Dollars More
d) Hang 'Em High

195 Which 1960 thriller starred Janet Leigh and Anthony Perkins at the Bates Motel?

    a) Vertigo   c) North by Northwest
    b) Psycho   d) The Birds

196 What was the name of the comedy variety program that writer Rob Petrie and colleagues Buddy and Sally worked on?

    a) The Dick Van Dyke Show   c) The Jerry Lewis Show
    b) The Alan Brady Show   d) The Andy Williams Show

FLASHBACK FACT

The Petries' "148 Bonnie Meadow Road" was inspired by creator Carl Reiner's real address, he just added a "1" to keep fans from stopping by. Today, the street has an honorary name: "Dick Van Dyke Show Way."

197 Which popular remote-controlled robot toy from the 1960s was marketed by the Ideal Toy Company and could walk, flash its lights, and fire miniature missiles?

a) Robot Commando   c) Big Loo
b) Mr. Machine   d) Robby the Robot

198 Which 1963 war film starred Steve McQueen as a motorcycle-riding Allied soldier?

a) Rio Bravo   c) The Cincinnati Kid
b) The Great Escape   d) The Sand Pebbles

199 Which 1969 film featured John Wayne winning his only Oscar for playing one-eyed marshal Rooster Cogburn?

a) True Grit   c) Rio Bravo
b) The Searchers   d) The Man Who Shot
                             Liberty Valance

200 Which magazine got a daring makeover in the 1960s and started embracing style and independence sparking a new era of women's media?

    a) Glamour   c) Seventeen
    b) Cosmopolitan   d) Vogue

201 Which 1967 variety show became a TV staple thanks to its hilarious comedy sketches, famous "ear tug" sign-offs, and a cast that could barely keep a straight face?

    a) The Carol Burnett Show   c) The Jackie Gleason Show
    b) The Dean Martin Show   d) The Ed Sullivan Show

202 Which dance craze popularized by Chubby Checker in 1960 had everyone spinning their hips?

    a) The Mashed Potato   c) The Watusi
    b) The Twist   d) The Monkey

203 Which 1964 Beatles film featured a famous scene of the Fab Four goofing around in a field while "Can't Buy Me Love" played?

a) Help!

c) Yellow Submarine

b) A Hard Day's Night

d) Magical Mystery Tour

FLASHBACK FACT

A Hard Day's Night was shot in just six weeks and on such a tight budget that many supporting actors were actual fans hanging around the set.

204 Which chewy fruit candy, first sold in the U.K. as "Opal Fruits" in 1960, made its U.S. debut in 1967 under a new name?

a) Starburst

c) Now and Later

b) Skittles

d) Jolly Rancher

205 Which 1968 comedy film starred Jack Lemmon and Walter Matthau as mismatched roommates?

a) The Odd Couple
b) The Fortune Cookie

c) The Front Page
d) Grumpy Old Men

206 Which children's cereal, introduced in 1963, featured a mustachioed sea captain who bragged about how crunchy it stayed, even in milk?

a) Popeye Cereal
b) Cap'n Crunch

c) Admiral Halsey's
d) Sailor Sam's

207 Which 1963 film featured Elizabeth Taylor and Richard Burton in an epic portrayal of the Egyptian queen?

a) Ben-Hur
b) Cleopatra

c) Lawrence of Arabia
d) Doctor Zhivago

208 Which super-bouncy toy sparked a mid-'60s craze after chemist Norman Stingley created its ultra-springy material?

a) Super Ball
b) Koosh Ball

c) Hacky Sack
d) Wonder Bubbles

209 Which 1967 film featured Paul Newman as a rebellious prisoner who famously said, "What we've got here is failure to communicate"?

a) The Hustler
b) Cool Hand Luke

c) Butch Cassidy and the Sundance Kid
d) Hud

210 Which 1964 Bond adventure made the Aston Martin DB5 a pop-culture icon?

a) From Russia with Love
b) Goldfinger

c) Here is 007
d) Thunderball

211 Which 1969 film featured Peter Fonda and Dennis Hopper on a cross-country motorcycle journey?

a) The Wild Angels
b) Easy Rider

c) Hell's Angels on Wheels
d) The Born Losers

212 Which game show, hosted by Monty Hall, debuted in 1963 and featured contestants choosing between doors?

a) The Price is Right
b) Let's Make a Deal

c) What's My Line?
d) To Tell the Truth

213 Which 1965 film starred Omar Sharif and Julie Christie in an epic Russian love story?

a) Lawrence of Arabia
b) Doctor Zhivago

c) Nicholas and Alexandra
d) War and Peace

FLASHBACK FACT

Only in Hollywood - Barbra Streisand and Katharine Hepburn tied for Best Actress in 1968, each taking home an Oscar for Funny Girl and The Lion in Winter.

214 Which 1968 sci-fi film featured Charlton Heston discovering the ruins of the Statue of Liberty?

a) Fantastic Voyage
b) Planet of the Apes
c) Forbidden Planet
d) The Time Machine

215 Which colorful fashion trend became a DIY craze in the late 1960s, thanks to hippie culture and music festivals?

a) Tie-dye
b) Batik
c) Sequin tops
d) The Flip

216 Which 1960 film featured Frank Sinatra, Dean Martin, and the rest of the "Rat Pack" planning a Las Vegas heist?

a) Ocean's 11
b) Sergeants 3

c) 4 for Texas
d) Robin and the 7 Hoods

217 Which 1968 zombie film by George Romero revolutionized horror movies?

a) Night of the Living Dead
b) The Cabinet of Dr. Caligari

c) Dawn of the Dead
d) The Texas Chainsaw Massacre

218 Which 1968 film featured Barbra Streisand in her Oscar-winning debut as comedienne Fanny Brice?

a) Hello, Dolly!
b) Funny Girl

c) The Way We Were
d) What's Up, Doc?

219 Which popular candy introduced in 1962 featured small, tart, colorful pieces that "made your mouth pucker"?

a) Mike and Ike

c) Runts

b) Nerds

d) Lemonhead

220 Which sitcom debuted in 1964 and featured a witch who twitched her nose to cast spells?

a) I Dream of Jeannie

c) The Flying Nun

b) Bewitched

d) That Girl

221 Which 1966 Beach Boys album featured the hit "Wouldn't It Be Nice"?

a) Sunflower

c) Pet Sounds

b) Wild Honey

d) Summer Days (And Summer Nights!!)

222 Which glowing decor item, introduced in 1963, featured wax blobs rising and falling in liquid?

a) Snow Globe

b) Water Wiggle

c) Whirly Wheel

d) Lava Lamp

223 Which famously bizarre and poorly-received sitcom from 1965 featured a central character driving a vintage 1928 automobile named "Porter"?

a) Knight Rider

b) My Mother the Car

c) The Jetsons

d) Mister Ed

224 Which slogan, popularized by the 1960s counterculture, became a rallying cry for peace during the anti-war movement?

a) "Make Love, Not War"

b) "Power to the People"

c) "Hell No, We Won't Go"

d) "Give Peace a Chance"

FLASHBACK FACT

Samantha's "nose twitch" wasn't special effects. Elizabeth Montgomery had a natural lip twitch she did when annoyed. Her husband, director William Asher, spotted it and turned it into TV magic, creating one of the most charming "spells" in sitcom history.

225 Which 1960s game challenged kids to create the longest dangling chain without dropping a piece, using nothing but plastic animals and steady hands?

a) Barrel of Monkeys   c) Jungle Jumble
b) Monkey Madness   d) Tree Topple

226 Which soul legend turned "Respect" into a 1967 anthem for empowerment, spelling out her message letter by letter?

a) Diana Ross   c) Etta James
b) Aretha Franklin   d) Tina Turner

227 Which animated series debuted in 1960 and featured a prehistoric family with a pet dinosaur named Dino?

a) The Jetsons
b) The Flintstones
c) Scooby-Doo
d) Yogi Bear

228 Which late-'60s fashion accessory swung its way through music festivals, featuring colorful beads, peace signs, and flower power vibes?

a) Friendship bracelets
b) Mood rings
c) Hippie necklaces
d) Tie-dye scarves

229 Which 1963 thriller starred Audrey Hepburn and Cary Grant in a suspenseful tale of murder and mistaken identity?

a) North by Northwest
b) Charade
c) How to Steal a Million
d) My Fair Lady

230 Which snack, introduced in 1967, featured a chocolatey spiral and cream filling that made it a lunchbox legend?

a) Ding Dongs
b) Ho Hos
c) Twinkies
d) Moon Pies

231 Which 1966 dance craze swept teen parties and TV shows, with dancers flailing their arms and legs in a quick, snappy rhythm?

a) The Twist
b) The Jerk
c) The Mashed Potato
d) The Monkey

232 Which catchphrase from the late '60s variety show Rowan & Martin's Laugh-In became a nationwide sensation?

a) "Far out!"
b) "Sock it to me!"
c) "Right on!"
d) "Can you dig it?"

233 Which sitcom debuted in 1964 and featured a family living at 1313 Mockingbird Lane?

a) The Addams Family
b) The Munsters
c) Bewitched
d) I Dream of Jeannie

234 Which 1963 hit by The Ronettes opened with the famous line, "The night we met I knew I needed you so"?

a) Will You Love Me Tomorrow
b) He's So Fine
c) Then He Kissed Me
d) Be My Baby

FLASHBACK FACT

Fred Gwynne's Herman Munster costume weighed almost 40 pounds, but he still managed to sing, dance, and crack up the cast. The Munster Koach was built from three Model Ts and cost $18,000 which was pricier than most new cars in 1964!

235 Which toy, released in 1964, featured a plastic mold and goopy gel to make rubbery bugs and creatures?

a) Easy-Bake Oven

c) Slime Lab

b) Creepy Crawlers

d) Monster Maker

236 Which TV show debuted in 1967 and featured a nun who could fly thanks to her starched habit?

a) That Girl

c) Bewitched

b) The Flying Nun

d) Gidget

237 Which hairstyle, popular in 1963, featured a high, rounded shape often held in place with hairspray?

a) The Flip

c) The Shag

b) The Beehive

d) The Bob

238 Which 1966 party game had players twisting themselves into tangled, awkward positions on a plastic mat covered with colored circles, sparking both laughter and controversy?

a) Simon Says

b) Limbo

c) Twister

d) Red Light, Green Light

239 Who gave the '60s its folksy voice with the song "Blowin' in the Wind"?

a) Bob Dylan

b) Neil Young

c) Simon & Garfunkel

d) Johnny Cash

240 Which 1964 musical introduced moviegoers to a whimsical nanny who flew in with her umbrella and sang about a spoonful of sugar?

a) The Sound of Music

b) Mary Poppins

c) Chitty Chitty Bang Bang

d) Bedknobs and Broomsticks

241 Which game, released in 1965, featured a plastic dome and a button that made characters pop up randomly?

a) Pop-Up Pals

b) Trouble

c) Whack-a-Mole

d) Surprise Spinner

242 Which 1963 sitcom followed a nosy reporter who suddenly found himself with a very out-of-this-world houseguest?

a) My Favorite Martian

b) Lost in Space

c) The Jetsons

d) The Twilight Zone

243 Which 1965 Rolling Stones hit became their first #1 single in the United States?

a) Paint it Black

b) Get Off of My Cloud

c) Ruby Tuesday

d) (I Can't Get No) Satisfaction

244 Which soul legend brought the house down in 1965 with his explosive performance of "I Got You (I Feel Good)," complete with signature dance moves and shouts?

a) Marvin Gaye　　　　c) Otis Redding
b) James Brown　　　　d) Sam Cooke

FLASHBACK FACT

James Brown's legendary cape routine debuted at the 1964 T.A.M.I. Show. During "Please, Please, Please," he'd drop to his knees as if overcome, and his valet, Danny Ray, would drape a cape over his shoulders to lead him off only for Brown to fling it away and storm back to the mic. The routine repeated several times and became a signature part of his act.

245 Which toy, introduced in 1960, featured a plastic screen and knobs that let kids draw with aluminum powder?

a) Etch A Sketch　　　　c) Spirograph
b) Lite-Brite　　　　d) Magna Doodle

246 Which TV show debuted in 1964 and featured a talking dolphin?

a) Sea Hunt
b) Flipper

c) Gentle Ben
d) Lassie

247 Which candy, popular in the mid-'60s, featured sweet, flavored syrup contained inside a small, chewable wax bottle?

a) Pixy Stix
b) Nik-L-Nip

c) Fun Dip
d) Zotz

248 Who had a hit with "Mrs. Brown You've Got a Lovely Daughter" in 1965?

a) The Beatles
b) Herman's Hermits

c) The Monkees
d) The Hollies

249 Which 1964 Broadway musical, starring Carol Channing, became a smash hit with its big, brassy title number and elaborate staging?

a) Funny Girl

b) Hello, Dolly!

c) Mame

d) Fiddler on the Roof

250 Which 1960s film marks the Hammer Film Productions debut of the Frankenstein Monster's make-up most closely resembling the classic square-headed Universal design, and featured wrestler Kiwi Kingston in the creature role?

a) Frankenstein Must Be Destroyed

b) The Evil of Frankenstein

c) The Bride of Frankenstein

d) Frankenstein Created Woman

Boogie Into the '70s

The 1970s were bold, funky, and unforgettable. Disco balls lit up Saturday nights while bell-bottoms, mood rings, and platform shoes ruled the closets. Kids begged for Pet Rocks and Star Wars action figures, teens tuned in to The Brady Bunch and Happy Days, and everyone lined up to see Jaws on the big screen. Music blasted on vinyl and 8-tracks, whether you were grooving to disco, cranking up rock, or swaying to singer-songwriters. Pong brought video games into living rooms, and the Bicentennial decked America in red, white, and blue. It was a decade of fads, fun, and cultural shift, so dust off that lava lamp, drop the needle on a Bee Gees record, and test how much you remember about the far-out '70s!

251 Which 1975 Broadway musical told the story of dancers auditioning for a show and featured the song "One"?

a) A Chorus Line
b) Cabaret
c) Chicago
d) Fame

252 Which 1970s sitcom featured the Fonzie character who could start jukeboxes with his fist?

a) Laverne & Shirley
b) Happy Days
c) Welcome Back, Kotter
d) What's Happening!!

253 Which Bee Gees disco anthem became forever linked to John Travolta's iconic strut through the streets of Brooklyn in Saturday Night Fever (1977)?

a) Night Fever
b) Stayin' Alive
c) Jive Talkin'
d) More Than a Woman

254 Which massive nationwide party took place in 1976 to blow out the candles on the nation's 200th birthday cake?

a) The Apollo–Soyuz Test Project

b) The Bicentennial

c) The Moon Landing Anniversary

d) Earth Day

255 Which 1972 arcade game turned two paddles and a bouncing dot into a worldwide craze, becoming the first commercially successful video game?

a) Space Invaders

b) Pong

c) Asteroids

d) Breakout

256 Which 1977 home console turned TV sets into gaming hubs with its revolutionary swappable cartridges and later hit titles like Space Invaders?

a) Gameboy

b) Atari 2600

c) Nintendo Entertainment System

d) Sega

257 Which TV family called 4222 Clinton Way in Los Angeles home, complete with a staircase perfect for family sing-alongs and plenty of sibling drama?

a) The Partridge Family
b) The Brady Bunch
c) Eight Is Enough
d) Good Times

258 Which rock band's 1973 hit 'Money' famously used a loop of cash registers and coins spliced from tape?

a) Led Zeppelin
b) Pink Floyd
c) The Who
d) The Rolling Stones

259 What was the name of the first U.S. space station, launched in 1973 to give astronauts a new kind of "home away from home" in orbit?

a) Skylab
b) Apollo 17
c) Voyager
d) Pioneer 10

260 Which 1978 musical film followed the summer romance between Sandy and Danny, complete with drive-in dates, leather jackets, and plenty of singing?

a) Fame

b) Grease

c) Saturday Night Fever

d) Hair

FLASHBACK FACT

Grease became the highest-grossing movie musical up to that time. Olivia Newton-John was 29 playing a high school senior, while John Travolta was 23. That is movie magic, baby!

261 Which 1979 film opened with Kermit singing "Rainbow Connection"?

a) The Great Muppet Caper

b) The Muppet Movie

c) Emmet Otter's Jug-Band Christmas

d) The Frog Prince

262 Which quirky 1975 fad came in a cardboard carrier with air holes?

a) Magic 8-Ball

b) Pet Rock

c) Rubik's Cube

d) Tamagotchi

263 Which 1975 thriller made audiences afraid to go in the water and gave us Roy Scheider's perfectly improvised warning: "You're gonna need a bigger boat"?

a) Orca

b) Jaws

c) The Deep

d) Piranha

264 Who became U.S. president after Richard Nixon resigned in 1974?

a) Gerald Ford

b) Jimmy Carter

c) Spiro Agnew

d) Ronald Reagan

265 Which 1970 Simon & Garfunkel hit begins, "When you're weary, feeling small..."?

a) The Boxer
b) Scarborough Fair

c) Bridge Over Troubled Water
d) Mrs. Robinson

266 Which 1979 Sony gadget let music lovers jog, commute, and hang out with their favorite tunes on the go, thanks to its lightweight headphones?

a) Boom box
b) Walkman

c) 8-track player
d) Transistor radio

267 Which 1977 TV miniseries captivated the nation, drawing record-breaking audiences over eight nights with its powerful multigenerational story?

a) Roots
b) Shōgun

c) Holocaust
d) Rich Man, Poor Man

268 Which musical genre dominated mid-to-late '70s charts with acts like Donna Summer and KC and the Sunshine Band?

a) Rock

b) Disco

c) Punk

d) Folk

269 Which long-running sketch comedy show premiered in 1975 with Chevy Chase and Gilda Radner?

a) MADtv

b) The Carol Burnett Show

c) Saturday Night Live

d) Laugh-In

FLASHBACK FACT

In 1976, SNL producer Lorne Michaels held up a $3,000 check on live TV, begging the Beatles to reunite. John Lennon and Paul McCartney were actually watching together in New York and later admitted they almost grabbed a cab to 30 Rock to crash the show!

270 Which magical 1971 film follows a poor boy who wins a Golden Ticket to tour the factory of an eccentric candy maker played by Gene Wilder?

a) Bedknobs and Broomsticks

b) Chitty Chitty Bang Bang

c) Willy Wonka & the Chocolate Factory

d) Charlotte's Web

271 Which spacecraft, launched in 1977 with a "Golden Record" of Earth sounds, is now sending data back from beyond our solar system?

a) Apollo 13

b) Voyager 1

c) Mariner 9

d) Pioneer 11

272 Which famous 1976 sports drama tells the story of an unknown, small-time club fighter from Philadelphia who gets an improbable shot at the heavyweight championship?

a) Raging Bull

b) Rocky

c) The Champ

d) Cinderella Man

273 Which '70s accessory claimed to reveal emotions through shifting colors?

a) Friendship bracelet

b) Mood ring

c) Pet Rock pendant

d) Tie-dye scarf

274 Which film won the 1972 Academy Award for Best Picture, starring Marlon Brando as a mafia boss?

a) The Godfather

b) Serpico

c) Taxi Driver

d) Mean Streets

275 Which car, introduced in 1970, became famous for its "Hemi" engine and high-performance muscle car status?

a) Chevrolet Camaro

b) Pontiac Firebird

c) AMC Gremlin

d) Dodge Challenger

276 Which 1973 attraction in Florida let guests get up close to orcas and other sea life?

a) Magic Kingdom
b) SeaWorld Orlando
c) Wet 'n Wild Orlando
d) Busch Gardens Tampa Bay

277 Which activity became a national craze in the 1970s, with disco lights, funky fashion, and smooth moves on four wheels?

a) Breakdancing
b) Hacky sack
c) Roller skating
d) Skateboarding

278 Which 1979 sci-fi horror film was advertised with the line, "In space no one can hear you scream"?

a) Alien
b) The Thing
c) Solaris
d) Outland

279 What 1973 event caused long lines at U.S. gas stations?

    a) Truckers' strike   c) Steel shortage

    b) Oil embargo   d) Airline crisis

280 Which Queen song with an operatic midsection became a '70s rock anthem?

    a) We Will Rock You   c) Bohemian Rhapsody

    b) Killer Queen   d) Somebody to Love

FLASHBACK FACT

When Bohemian Rhapsody first hit radio in 1975, DJs worried it was "too long" at six minutes. Fans begged for it anyway, calling stations nonstop until it became a worldwide hit.

281 Which 1978 Milton Bradley electronic memory game challenged players to repeat flashing light and sound patterns?

a) Simon
b) Speak & Spell
c) Merlin
d) Operation

282 Which mid-1970s craze had Americans installing antennas on their cars and saying things like "Breaker, breaker 1-9"?

a) Laser tag
b) Pong tournaments
c) CB radio boom
d) UFO spotting clubs

283 Which 1977 album by Fleetwood Mac became one of the decade's biggest sellers?

a) Tusk
b) Rumours
c) Mirage
d) Tango in the Night

284 In which gritty 1976 film does Robert De Niro stare into a mirror and improvise the unforgettable line, "You talkin' to me?"

a) Mean Streets   c) Serpico
b) Taxi Driver   d) Dog Day Afternoon

285 Which 1976 arcade game from Atari had players controlling a paddle to break rows of bricks?

a) Asteroids   c) Galaxian
b) Breakout   d) Pong

286 Which 1974 film by Mel Brooks spoofed old horror movies and featured the line, "It's pronounced Fronkensteen"?

a) Blazing Saddles   c) Starman
b) Young Frankenstein   d) Silent Running

287 Which home computer, released in 1977, helped kick-start the personal computing craze?

a) IBM PC

b) Apple II

c) Amiga 1000

d) Macintosh

288 What nuclear accident occurred near Harrisburg, Pennsylvania, in 1979?

a) Chernobyl

b) Three Mile Island

c) Windscale

d) Fukushima

289 Which 1975 candy caused an urban legend that it could be dangerous when eaten with soda?

a) Nerds

b) Pop Rocks

c) Fun Dip

d) Warheads

290 Which superhero TV series starring Lynda Carter debuted in 1975?

a) The Bionic Woman
b) Wonder Woman

c) The Incredible Hulk
d) Shazam!

FLASHBACK FACT

Lynda Carter came up with Wonder Woman's famous spin transformation herself. The producers loved it and kids everywhere were twirling in their living rooms, hoping to turn into superheroes too!

291 Which tabletop role-playing game created by Gary Gygax and Dave Arneson premiered in 1974?

a) Traveller
b) Car Wars

c) Dungeons & Dragons
d) RuneQuest

292 Which 1976 red-swimsuit poster turned a TV star into a national sensation, selling millions of copies and decorating countless bedroom walls?

a) Cheryl Tiegs
b) Farrah Fawcett
c) Raquel Welch
d) Loni Anderson

293 Which U.S. law passed in 1972 prohibited sex discrimination in education programs receiving federal funds?

a) Title VII
b) Title IX
c) Equal Pay Act
d) ERA

294 Which hit sitcom spun off from All in the Family and premiered in 1975?

a) Maude
b) The Jeffersons
c) Good Times
d) Archie Bunker's Place

295 Which 1978 horror film set in Haddonfield launched a long-running slasher franchise?

a) Friday the 13th　　c) The Omen
b) Halloween　　d) Phantasm

296 Which 1975 Bruce Springsteen single turned the open road into pure poetry?

a) Thunder Road　　c) Badlands
b) Born to Run　　d) Rosalita

297 Which 1975 cult comedy followed King Arthur on an extremely silly quest?

a) Life of Brian　　c) Monty Python and
b) Time Bandits　　the Holy Grail
d) Jabberwocky

298 Which supersonic airliner began commercial service in 1976, crossing the Atlantic at about Mach 2?

a) Tu-144

c) Boeing 2707

b) Concorde

d) DC-10

299 Which 1979 Atari arcade game let players pilot a spaceship, blasting drifting asteroids in a crisp vector-graphics universe?

a) Super Breakout

c) Centipede

b) Asteroids

d) Battlezone

300 Which educational TV shorts began in 1973, teaching with songs like "I'm Just a Bill"?

a) The Electric Company

c) Sesame Street shorts

d) Time for Timer

b) Schoolhouse Rock!

FLASHBACK FACT

Jack Sheldon, the jazz musician who voiced "I'm Just a Bill," also played trumpet on The Merv Griffin Show. Kids (and adults too) sang along without realizing the catchy civics lesson was delivered by a real jazzman.

301 Which sitcom, debuting in 1972, starred Bea Arthur as a sharp-tongued feminist and Edith Bunker's cousin?

a) The Jeffersons   c) Maude
b) Good Times   d) One Day at a Time

302 Which rock band released Hotel California in 1976?

a) The Rolling Stones   c) Fleetwood Mac
b) The Eagles   d) The Doobie Brothers

303 Which U.S. national park, famous for its jagged peaks, turquoise lakes, and the scenic Going-to-the-Sun Road, was designated a National Wilderness Area in 1975?

a) Yellowstone
b) Glacier
c) Yosemite
d) Petrified Forest

304 Which 1979 comedy film by Steve Martin featured him as a clueless but lovable character who becomes "somebody" after finding his name in the phone book?

a) Staying Alive
b) Being There
c) Animal House
d) The Jerk

305 Which 1976 album by the Ramones helped define punk rock?

a) Never Mind the Bollocks
b) Ramones
c) London Calling
d) Rocket to Russia

306 What 1979 film featured Mel Gibson as "Mad" Max Rockatansky?

a) The Road Warrior
b) Mad Max
c) Escape from New York
d) Death Race 2000

307 Which 1977 NASA program launched two spacecraft carrying the Golden Record which was a time capsule of Earth's music, greetings, and sounds, into deep space?

a) Voyager
b) Apollo-Soyuz
c) Pioneer
d) Skylab

308 Which 1974 Carl Douglas hit became a surprise #1 with its disco beat and martial arts theme?

a) Kung Fu Fighting
b) Play That Funky Music
c) Car Wash
d) Superfly

309 Which sitcom, debuting in 1976, followed two roommates working at a Milwaukee brewery?

a) Alice

b) Happy Days

c) Laverne & Shirley

d) Diff'rent Strokes

310 What 1977 film, directed by George Lucas, introduced audiences to R2-D2 and C-3PO?

a) Star Trek: The Motion Picture

b) Star Wars

c) Battlestar Galactica

d) Flash Gordon

FLASHBACK FACT

The lightsaber's iconic hum was pure '70s DIY. Sound designer Ben Burtt mixed the motor of an old movie projector with the buzz from a broken mic cable to create one of cinema's most legendary sounds.

311 Which 1978 comic strip by Jim Davis introduced a lasagna-loving cat?

a) Heathcliff

b) Garfield

c) B.C.

d) The Far Side

312 Which 1970s pop artist turned Chairman Mao into a neon-colored, commercial-art superstar, blending politics and pop culture in bold, bright prints?

a) Andy Warhol

b) Roy Lichtenstein

c) Keith Haring

d) Pablo Picasso

313 Which PBS show, debuting in 1971, featured animated shorts and sketches teaching kids about reading?

a) Reading Rainbow

b) The Electric Company

c) Zoom

d) 3-2-1 Contact

320 Which 1979 disco hit by Gloria Gaynor became an anthem of resilience?

a) Don't Leave Me This Way

b) I Will Survive

c) We Are Family

d) Last Dance

FLASHBACK FACT

"I Will Survive" was never meant to be the star; it was stuck on the B-side of "Substitute." But club DJs flipped the record, dance floors went wild, and Gloria Gaynor's anthem of resilience became disco history.

321 Which 1970s sitcom starred Redd Foxx as a junk dealer in Los Angeles?

a) Sanford and Son

b) Taxi

c) One Day at a Time

d) Good Times

322 Which ABC miniseries dramatized life in the American West and starred Richard Chamberlain?

a) Roots
b) Centennial
c) Rich Man, Poor Man
d) Winds of War

323 Which 1978 blockbuster's special effects were considered groundbreaking for the decade, featuring wirework, front projection, and flying sequences, starring a character who hides his identity as a journalist by day?

a) Superman
b) Flash Gordon
c) Batman
d) Spider-Man

324 Which 1976 Stevie Wonder album won the Grammy for Album of the Year?

a) Songs in the Key of Life
b) Innervisions
c) Talking Book
d) Hotter than July

325 Which 1978 arcade hit by Taito launched the golden age of video games, letting players defend Earth from rows of descending aliens?

a) Super Breakout
b) Asteroids

c) Space Invaders
d) Defender

326 Which 1973 sci-fi film feeds the masses with a mysterious new food... until someone finds out what's really on the menu?

a) Logan's Run
b) Soylent Green

c) The Omega Man
d) Westworld

327 Which 1976 game show, hosted by Chuck Barris, featured contestants performing bizarre, funny, or shocking acts for celebrity judges, with the possibility of being stopped mid-performance?

a) The Dating Game
b) The Gong Show

c) Match Game
d) Hollywood Squares

328 Which singer released the 1971 album Tapestry, featuring "It's Too Late" and "You've Got a Friend"?

a) Carly Simon

b) Carole King

c) Joni Mitchell

d) Linda Ronstadt

329 Which 1972 home video game console let people play games on their own TVs for the first time, complete with simple graphics, cards, and plastic overlays to turn your screen into a game board?

a) Atari 2600

b) Magnavox Odyssey

c) ColecoVision

d) Fairchild Channel F

330 Which 1974 blockbuster disaster film had audiences on the edge of their seats as a fire raged through the world's tallest skyscraper, with star-studded heroes racing to save the day?

a) The Towering Inferno

b) Earthquake

c) Airport

d) Close Encounters

331 Which 1977 miniseries about corruption and journalism starred Robert Blake and was based on a novel by John Ehrlichman?

a) Centennial
b) Rich Man, Poor Man
c) Washington: Behind Closed Doors
d) Winds of War

FLASHBACK FACT

The finale of Roots in 1977 drew over 100 million viewers which was more than that year's Super Bowl. For eight nights, a TV miniseries united the nation and made history.

332 What 1975 sitcom starred Sherman Hemsley and Isabel Sanford as a couple who "moved on up to the East Side"?

a) Diff'rent Strokes
b) The Jeffersons
c) Maude
d) Good Times

333 Which 1972 Olympic basketball game ended in chaos with confusion, multiple clock stoppages, and a final play that left fans and players debating for decades?

a) USA vs. USSR

b) USA vs. Yugoslavia

c) USSR vs. Italy

d) USA vs. Canada

334 Which 1979 sci-fi comedy had the Monty Python troupe hilariously poking fun at biblical epics, following a man who's constantly mistaken for a Messiah?

a) Jabberwocky

b) Life of Brian

c) Time Bandits

d) Yellowbeard

335 Which 1976 film stars Robert Redford and Dustin Hoffman as reporters digging into a massive political scandal, showing how journalism uncovered the Watergate conspiracy?

a) Network

b) The Paper Chase

c) All the President's Men

d) The Candidate

336 Which candy bar was introduced to the U.S. market in 1979, featuring two biscuit fingers covered in caramel and chocolate?

a) Twix

b) Kit Kat

c) 100 Grand

d) Milky Way

337 Which iconic disco group, known for their elaborate costumes featuring a construction worker, a cowboy, a cop, and an Indian chief, had a smash hit with "Y.M.C.A."?

a) KC and the Sunshine Band

b) The Village People

c) Earth, Wind & Fire

d) The Bee Gees

338 Which groundbreaking 1970 book by Judy Blume was challenged in schools for its frank talk on adolescence?

a) Forever...

b) Blubber

c) Are You There God? It's Me, Margaret

d) Then Again, Maybe I Won't

339 Which baseball player broke Babe Ruth's career home run record in 1974?

a) Reggie Jackson
b) Hank Aaron

c) Willie Mays
d) Pete Rose

340 Which 1978 Broadway musical featured the song "Ease on Down the Road" and later became a film starring Diana Ross?

a) Dreamgirls
b) The Wiz

c) Pippin
d) A Chorus Line

FLASHBACK FACT

Michael Jackson's first movie role was as the Scarecrow in The Wiz (1978). Even better? That's where he met Quincy Jones, who went on to produce Off the Wall, Thriller, and Bad – the hit trilogy that crowned Jackson the King of Pop.

341 Which 1976 thriller by Stephen King became a hit film starring Sissy Spacek?

a) The Shining
b) Carrie
c) Salem's Lot
d) Firestarter

342 Which 1972 TV show followed Hawkeye and friends working in a mobile army hospital in Korea?

a) M*A*S*H*
b) Hogan's Heroes
c) The Rat Patrol
d) Emergency!

343 Which 1979 comedy, co-written by Harold Ramis, featured Bill Murray as a camp counselor?

a) Animal House
b) Meatballs
c) Stripes
d) Caddyshack

344 Which classic rock opera by The Who was later adapted into a 1975 film featuring an all-star cast (including Roger Daltrey, Elton John, Tina Turner, and Jack Nicholson) and tells the story of a "deaf, dumb, and blind" messiah?

a) Quadrophenia

c) A Quick One

b) Tommy

d) Live at Leeds

345 Which 1974 sitcom followed a strong, no-nonsense mom raising her kids with humor and resilience in Chicago's Cabrini-Green housing project?

a) Good Times

c) What's Happening!!

b) Sanford and Son

d) One Day at a Time

346 Which 1977 Donna Summer track made dancers feel like they'd stepped onto a futuristic disco floor, with hypnotic synths and mirrorball magic?

a) I Feel Love

c) Hot Stuff

b) Last Dance

d) Love to Love You Baby

347 Which 1976 film featured Peter Finch shouting, "I'm mad as hell, and I'm not going to take this anymore!"?

a) Network
b) Serpico
c) All the President's Men
d) Dog Day Afternoon

348 Which 1976 miniseries starred Nick Nolte and Peter Strauss as brothers on opposite sides of society?

a) Centennial
b) Rich Man, Poor Man
c) Captains and the Kings
d) Roots

349 Which 1979 doll line brought a gang of fruity, colorful characters to life, complete with scented hair and accessories, cupcakes, and a world of sugary adventures?

a) Strawberry Shortcake
b) Cabbage Patch Kids
c) Holly Hobbie
d) Rainbow Brite

350 Which 1976 miniseries starred Nick Nolte and Peter Strauss as brothers on opposite sides of society?

a) Centennial

b) Rich Man, Poor Man

c) Captains and the Kings

d) Roots

351 Which 1978 science series hosted by James Burke connected inventions across history into surprising chains?

a) Cosmos

b) Nova

c) The Ascent of Man

d) Connections

FLASHBACK FACT

James Burke once took viewers on an unforgettable ride, starting with a simple plow, zigzagging through centuries of discoveries, and ending with a rocket on the moon. It felt like watching the greatest connect-the-dots puzzle ever come to life.

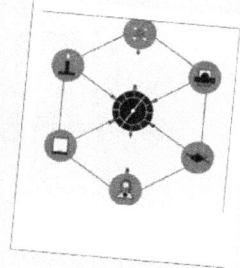

352 Which 1970s sitcom starred a clever Associate Producer at a Minneapolis TV station, juggling deadlines, eccentric coworkers, and a hilariously self-important news anchor?

a) Rhoda

b) The Mary Tyler Moore Show

c) One Day at a Time

d) Phyllis

353 Which 1973 Roberta Flack hit wrapped audiences in soulful, goosebump-inducing vocals and went on to win the Grammy for Record of the Year?

a) You've Got a Friend

b) Time in a Bottle

c) The First Time I Ever Saw Your Face

d) Killing Me Softly with His Song

354 Which 1978 Chic hit blasted out of speakers at Studio 54, sending dancers into a frenzy with its irresistible groove and a shout-along refrain that took over the dance floor?

a) Boogie Wonderland

b) Le Freak

c) Celebration

d) Don't Stop 'Til You Get Enough

355 Which 1970 NASA mission suffered a mid-flight oxygen tank explosion, sparking the famous "Houston, we've had a problem" moment, and pulled off a daring return to Earth that had the world holding its breath?

a) Apollo 11

b) Apollo 13

c) Apollo 14

d) Apollo 15

356 Which 1974 country hit by Dolly Parton was later re-recorded in the 1990s by Whitney Houston for a blockbuster film?

a) Jolene

b) I Will Always Love You

c) Coat of Many Colors

d) 9 to 5

357 Which 1978 sci-fi TV series introduced viewers to Captain Apollo, epic space battles, and the villainous Cylons, blending Star Wars-era spectacle with weekly TV drama?

a) Battlestar Galactica

b) Buck Rogers

c) Space: 1999

d) Star Trek: The Animated Series

358 Which 1972 live gospel album captured Aretha Franklin at the height of her powers, recorded in a Los Angeles church and later hailed as one of the greatest performances of her career?

a) Spirit in the Dark

b) Amazing Grace

c) Lady Soul

d) Young, Gifted and Black

359 Which 1975 film follows Jack Nicholson as a rebellious troublemaker who shakes up life inside a psychiatric hospital, clashing with the unforgettable Nurse Ratched?

a) Chinatown

b) One Flew Over the Cuckoo's Nest

c) Five Easy Pieces

d) Terms of Endearment

360 Which 1978 sitcom introduced TV audiences to Robin Williams as a wild, fast-talking alien from Ork who moves in with a young woman in Colorado and gave us the unforgettable catchphrase "Na-nu Na-nu"?

a) Perfect Strangers

b) Mork & Mindy

c) Laverne & Shirley

d) Taxi

FLASHBACK FACT

During the filming of The Mary Tyler Moore Show's opening credits, Mary really did toss her hat in the air on a busy Minneapolis street and a bystander rushed over, thinking she needed help! The moment became so iconic that TV Land later built a bronze statue of Mary mid-hat toss downtown.

The Totally Awesome '80s

The 1980s were loud, bright, and unforgettable. MTV made music videos must-see TV, arcades buzzed with Pac-Man fever, and Saturday mornings meant cartoons and cereal. Kids begged for Cabbage Patch Kids and Transformers, teens lived by their mixtapes and Walkmans, and everyone lined up for E.T., Back to the Future, and The Breakfast Club. Fashion was big; neon, leg warmers, and sky-high hair; and the music had just as much attitude. From Michael Jackson's moonwalk to Rubik's Cube showdowns, the '80s were a decade of color, energy, and totally awesome memories. Slip on those high-tops, press play on your boombox, and see how well you remember the '80s!

361 Which furry alien from the planet Melmac crash-landed in the Tanner family's garage in 1986?

a) E.T.

b) Alf

c) Gizmo

d) Mork

362 Which 1980 arcade game had players munching pellets and dodging colorful ghosts?

a) Donkey Kong

b) Pac-Man

c) Frogger

d) Space Invaders

363 Which colorful binder with Velcro flaps and pockets became a school-supply status symbol?

a) Lisa Frank Folders

b) Trapper Keeper

c) Pee-Chee Portfolio

d) Mead Spiral Notebook

364 What 1981 arcade hit first introduced Mario (then "Jumpman") as he tried to save Pauline from an ape?

a) Donkey Kong

b) Super Mario Bros.

c) BurgerTime

d) Q*bert

365 Which pouch gum launched in 1980 let kids "chew like the pros" (minus the tobacco)?

a) Hubba Bubba

b) Bazooka

c) Big League Chew

d) Bubble Yum

366 Which bright, flexible plastic shoes became a summertime must-have for kids?

a) Crocs

b) Jellies

c) Converse

d) Vans

367 What wildly popular doll line came with a unique name, "adoption papers," and sparked a nationwide craze that had parents scrambling through toy aisles?

a) My Buddy

b) Care Bears

c) Cabbage Patch Kids

d) Pound Puppies

368 Which NBC sitcom, debuting in 1984, followed a spunky orphan and her dog Brandon?

a) Silver Spoons

b) Punky Brewster

c) Diff'rent Strokes

d) Webster

369 Which colorful fashion accessory from Switzerland became a collectible craze, with kids stacking multiples on one arm?

a) Casio Calculator Watch

b) Swatch Watch

c) Timex

d) Guess

370 Which collectible cards parodied cutesy dolls with gloriously gross humor?

a) Hogan's Alley

b) Duck Hunt

c) Wild Gunman

d) Clay Shooter

FLASHBACK FACT

Garbage Pail Kids were an '80s phenomenon and Topps sold over 800 million cards in just a few years. Lunchrooms turned into trading floors where the grosser the design, the higher the value.

371 Which NES light-gun game had players blasting at ducks on CRT TVs while a mischievous dog laughed when they missed?

a) Hogan's Alley

b) Duck Hunt

c) Wild Gunman

d) Clay Shooter

372 Which 1985 Nintendo classic whisked players into the Mushroom Kingdom to stomp Goombas, warp through pipes, and rescue Princess Toadstool from Bowser's clutches?

a) Super Mario Bros.
b) The Legend of Zelda
c) Metroid
d) Kid Icarus

373 Which 1980s electronic learning toy from VTech quizzed kids on spelling, math, and more with a glowing screen - basically the coolest "laptop" a kid could own back then?

a) Talking Whiz Kid
b) Speak & Spell
c) Simon
d) Merlin

374 Which soft, cozy socks became a major '80s fashion trend, often layered in bright colors over leggings or paired with high-top sneakers for that signature look?

a) Crew socks
b) Slouch socks
c) Tube socks
d) Knee socks

375 Which 1984 movie taught us three unforgettable rules about mysterious furry creatures: keep them out of bright light, don't get them wet, and never feed them after midnight?

a) E.T.

b) Gremlins

c) The Goonies

d) Short Circuit

376 Which 24-hour music channel launched in 1981 with the words "Ladies and gentlemen, rock and roll," forever changing pop culture with round-the-clock music videos?

a) VH1

b) MTV

c) MuchMusic

d) BET

377 Which Nickelodeon game show, debuting in 1986, had kids answering trivia, taking on messy stunts, and occasionally digging through a giant slime-filled nose to find the hidden flag on the obstacle course?

a) Finders Keepers

b) Double Dare

c) Guts

d) Legends of the Hidden Temple

378 Which 1984 puzzle game created by Alexey Pajitnov had players stacking falling shapes into perfect lines sparking a late-'80s global craze and becoming a Game Boy must-have?

a) Columns

b) Tetris

c) Dr. Mario

d) Qix

379 Which sneaker style, known for bold colors, oversized tongues, and Velcro or fat laces, ruled school hallways and playgrounds in the '80s?

a) Crocs

b) High-tops

c) Doc Martens

d) Jellies

380 Which beloved '80s cartoon featured magical bears with belly badges who lived in a cloud-top kingdom and spread love and cheer to kids everywhere?

a) Care Bears

b) My Little Pony

c) Rainbow Brite

d) Smurfs

381 Which game show had contestants spin a giant board for cash and prizes while dodging an animated troublemaker?

a) Card Sharks

b) Press Your Luck

c) Family Feud

d) Sale of the Century

FLASHBACK FACT

In 1984, contestant Michael Larson stunned viewers on Press Your Luck by memorizing the game board's light patterns and winning a record $110,237. Producers investigated, but he hadn't cheated, just outsmarted the system. Following this, the show changed the board's light pattern programming to prevent anyone from repeating his feat.

382 Who was the high-fashion dot-gobbler who stole Pac-Man's heart (and top leaderboard spot) in the 1982 sequel, easily identified by her signature hair bow and lipstick?

a) Pac-Man Jr.

b) Ms. Pac-Man

c) Dig Dug

d) Galaga

383 Which powdered drink mix brought the "Oh Yeah!" to birthday parties and backyard cookouts?

a) Kool-Aid
b) Capri Sun

c) Tang
d) Hi-C

384 Defined by the concept of "Friendship is Magic," what massive entertainment franchise centers on characters who each possess a unique symbol (or "Cutie Mark") that reflects their greatest talent?

a) Rainbow Brite
b) Strawberry Shortcake

c) My Little Pony
d) Popples

385 Which 1982 game console was Atari's big follow-up to the 2600, boasting better graphics, a fancy (but notoriously finicky) controller, and a bid to keep ahead in the console wars?

a) Atari 5200
b) Nintendo NES

c) Sega Master System
d) ColecoVision

386 Which board game, introduced in 1981, became a pop culture phenomenon by testing players' knowledge in categories like Arts & Literature and Sports & Leisure?

a) Trivial Pursuit

b) Pictionary

c) Scrabble

d) Scattergories

387 What was the name of the adorable Mogwai who became a pop culture icon from Gremlins?

a) Stripe

b) Gizmo

c) Yoda

d) Nibbles

FLASHBACK FACT

Gremlins was so intense it helped inspire the PG-13 rating (with a little help from Temple of Doom). Luckily, Gizmo stole hearts and soon, "Gizmo" became one of the most popular pet names in America.

388 Which 1985 adventure movie had kids searching for pirate treasure with the help of a map and "One-Eyed Willy"?

a) Explorers

b) Stand by Me

c) The Goonies

d) Labyrinth

389 Which budget-friendly, pocket-sized electronic games became a '90s craze with their single-game handhelds, featuring simple LCD screens, pre-printed backgrounds, and titles like Baseball and Football?

a) Nintendo Game Boy

b) Tiger Electronics

c) Milton Bradley Microvision

d) Atari Lynx

390 Which hit 1981 song by Journey opens with the iconic line, "Just a small town girl..."?

a) Separate Ways

b) Don't Stop Believin'

c) Faithfully

d) Wheel in the Sky

391 Which handheld puzzle toy drove kids (and adults) a little crazy in the '80s, as they twisted and turned, desperately trying to get all six sides to match?

a) Simon
b) Rubik's Cube
c) Perplexus
d) Magic Snake

392 Which late '80s squishy toy with soft, colorful rubber strands became a classroom craze that was ideal for tossing across the room when the teacher wasn't looking?

a) Stress Ball
b) Koosh Ball
c) Hacky Sack
d) Silly Putty

393 Which Nickelodeon show, debuting in 1981, made slime a messy legend by dumping it on kids whenever they innocently said, "I don't know"?

a) Double Dare
b) You Can't Do That on Television
c) Wild & Crazy Kids
d) Finders Keepers

394 Which 1980s TV show had David Hasselhoff, a talking supercar named KITT, and a glowing red scanner that meant business?

a) Knight Rider

b) Airwolf

c) The A-Team

d) CHiPs

395 Which "gross-out" toy line had rubbery monster balls with goofy faces, competing with Garbage Pail Kids for laughs?

a) My Pet Monster

b) Madballs

c) Creepy Crawlers

d) Boglins

396 Which early 1980s arcade game let players pilot a triangle-shaped ship while blasting waves of geometric enemies?

a) Tempest

b) Tron

c) Asteroids

d) Galaga

397 Which PBS painting show made "happy little trees" famous in the '80s?

a) Paint Along with Nancy

b) The Joy of Painting

c) Color World

d) Masterpiece Paints

398 Which 1987 Nintendo adventure game sent players across the land of Hyrule, battling monsters, exploring dungeons, and rescuing a captured princess?

a) Castlevania

b) The Legend of Zelda

c) Kid Icarus

d) Dragon Quest

399 Which 1985 John Hughes film followed a group of teens spending Saturday in detention?

a) Pretty in Pink

b) Sixteen Candles

c) The Breakfast Club

d) Ferris Bueller's Day Off

FLASHBACK FACT

Before Spotify playlists, we had the cassingle. For under $2, you could grab your favorite song on a cassette tape. Bonus: when it got tangled, you became a pro surgeon with a pencil.

400 Which toy line featured transforming robots from the planet Cybertron locked in an epic battle between Autobots and Decepticons?

a) GoBots   c) Voltron
b) Transformers   d) Robotech

401 Which basketball superstar, nicknamed "His Airness" for his gravity-defying moves, entered the NBA in 1984?

a) Magic Johnson   c) Michael Jordan
b) Larry Bird   d) Charles Barkley

402 Which parody master scored laughs in the 1980s with hits like "Eat It," a spoof of Michael Jackson's "Beat It"?

a) Chevy Chase
b) Billy Crystal

c) Eddie Murphy
d) "Weird Al" Yankovic

403 Which bizarre and beloved 1982 arcade game cast you as an underground miner who defeated enemies by either dropping rocks on them or inflating them with a pump until they popped?

a) Dig Dug
b) Centipede

c) Joust
d) Galaxian

404 Which fruity snack, introduced in 1983, let kids unpeel colorful sheets of chewy goodness straight from the backing?

a) Fruit Roll-Ups
b) String Thing

c) Fruit by the Foot
d) Twizzlers Pull 'n' Peel

405 Which 1980s animated series starred a blue lion-headed hero who wielded the Sword of Omens and led a team of feline warriors?

    a) He-Man   c) Voltron

    b) Thundercats   d) G.I. Joe

406 Which 1983 film featured Matthew Broderick as a teen hacker who accidentally accesses a military computer?

    a) Tron   c) The Last Starfighter

    b) Wargames   d) Hackers

407 Which gum brand used the catchy slogan "the taste that's gonna move ya" in its famous commercials?

    a) Juicy Fruit   c) Hubba Bubba

    b) Big Red   d) Bubble Yum

408 Which toy line featured tiny, rubbery wrestlers that kids collected in buckets?

a) M.U.S.C.L.E.

b) Madballs

c) Army Ants

d) Battle Beasts

409 Which 1985 sitcom featured four witty single women sharing late-night talks (and cheesecake) in their Miami home?

a) Designing Women

b) The Golden Girls

c) Kate & Allie

d) 227

410 Which popular 1980s summer footwear trend featured translucent, flexible material and came in a rainbow of bright colors?

a) Jellies

b) Crocs

c) Espadrilles

d) Vans

411 Which Texas Instruments toy, known for quizzing kids in a robotic voice, got its Hollywood moment helping E.T. "phone home"?

a) Alphie
b) Speak & Spell

c) Simon
d) Ask Zandar

412 Which '80s sitcom featured a conservative teen with a briefcase in hand and Reagan posters on the wall, growing up in a warm, liberal family?

a) Family Matters
b) Family Ties

c) Growing Pains
d) Silver Spoons

413 Which 1980s playground toy counted your jumps as you spun a plastic hoop around your ankle?

a) Skip-It
b) Moon Shoes

c) Pogo Ball
d) Hoppity Hop

414 Which arcade game featured an animal dodging traffic and hopping across logs to reach home?

a) Frogger

b) Q*bert

c) Dig Dug

d) Centipede

415 Which animatronic talking bear, introduced in 1985, read stories to kids using special cassette tapes?

a) Popples

b) Teddy Ruxpin

c) Rainbow Brite

d) My Buddy

416 Which 1980s reading incentive program at Pizza Hut rewarded kids with free personal pan pizzas?

a) Pizza Power

b) Book It!

c) Read Across America

d) Read for a Pie

417 Which sneaker brand made kids feel like basketball superstars by pumping up their shoes through a tiny orange ball on the tongue?

a) Reebok Pump

b) Nike Air

c) LA Gear

d) Converse

418 Which 1982 film gave us the unforgettable image of a bike flying across the moon with a special passenger in the basket?

a) Poltergeist

b) The Last Starfighter

c) The NeverEnding Story

d) E.T. the Extra-Terrestrial

FLASHBACK FACT

Trapper Keepers were so cool in the '80s that some schools actually banned them, claiming the Velcro made too much noise in class. Of course, that only made kids love them more. Suddenly, comparing your Trapper Keeper cover under the desk felt like an underground club.

419 Which '80s DIY fashion trend involved decorating safety pins with colorful beads and trading them with friends to wear on shoelaces?

a) Pogs
b) Friendship Pins
c) Buddy Bracelets
d) Jelly Pals

420 Which 1985 film starred Michael J. Fox as a teen who time-traveled in a DeLorean?

a) Teen Wolf
b) Weird Science
c) Back to the Future
d) Ferris Bueller's Day Off

421 Which Saturday morning cartoon featured a magical girl and her trusty horse Starlite, spreading color and cheer to a gray world?

a) Strawberry Shortcake
b) Rainbow Brite
c) Popples
d) Care Bears

422 Which console revived home gaming after the early '80s crash, powered by a plumber in red overalls?

a) Sega Master System
b) Nintendo Entertainment System

(NES)
c) Atari 7800
d) ColecoVision

423 Which 1986 fantasy film features a teen's quest through a magical maze to rescue her baby brother from a mysterious Goblin King?

a) Legend
b) Labyrinth

c) The Dark Crystal
d) Willow

424 Which chewing gum came in a soft, square pouch and promised big bubbles without sticking?

a) Hubba Bubba
b) Big League Chew

c) Double Bubble
d) Bazooka

FLASHBACK FACT

Hubba Bubba changed bubble gum forever with a special formula that made popped bubbles less likely to stick to your face or hair. It was the first "mistake-friendly" gum, perfect for rookie bubble blowers showing off at recess.

425 On Fraggle Rock, what were the names of the tiny, hardworking green creatures who were always busy building elaborate structures out of edible radish paste?

a) Frackles

b) The Silly Creatures

c) Doozers

d) Gorgs

426 Which sticky toy, often found as a cereal box prize, became a craze for the strange way it flopped and inched along surfaces after being thrown?

a) Koosh Ball

b) Wacky Wall Walkers

c) Silly Putty

d) Slime

427 Which 1981 arcade game featured a quirky character leaping across a pyramid of cubes, changing their colors while dodging pesky enemies like Coily the snake?

a) Q*bert

b) Frogger

c) Dig Dug

d) Centipede

428 Which '80s hair accessory was colorful, stretchy, and often matched your leggings?

a) Bandana

b) Scrunchie

c) Headband

d) Hair bow

429 Which 1980s fast food promotion gave away collectible drinking glasses featuring movie characters like the Muppets and E.T.?

a) Burger King

b) McDonald's

c) Pizza Hut

d) Wendy's

430 Before a certain blue hedgehog stole the spotlight, which 8-bit video game hero with a blue spiked haircut and red jumpsuit was Sega's mascot?

a) Donkey Kong
b) Sonic the Hedgehog
c) Kid Chameleon
d) Alex Kidd

431 Which toy line featured plush puppies that came in little cardboard "doghouses"?

a) Pound Puppies
b) Popples
c) Puppy Surprise
d) My Pet Monster

432 Which late-'80s sitcom followed a widowed dad raising three daughters in San Francisco with help from his best friend and his rock 'n' roll brother-in-law?

a) Growing Pains
b) Full House
c) Perfect Strangers
d) Charles in Charge

433 Which snap-happy fashion fad was banned in some schools after kids started injuring themselves with knockoff versions?

a) Jelly Bracelets   c) Friendship Pins
b) Slap Bracelets   d) Buddy Bands

434 Which 1980s toy let kids "make a splash" with a long plastic sheet sprayed with water from the hose?

a) Super Soaker   c) Sprinkler Run
b) Slip 'N Slide   d) Splash Pad

435 Which sitcom featured a college student who moved in to help wrangle the kids (and sometimes the parents) all while trying to finish school himself?

a) Charles in Charge   c) Head of the Class
b) Perfect Strangers   d) Growing Pains

436 Which 1984 martial arts film featured Mr. Miyagi teaching Daniel the ways of "wax on, wax off"?

a) Bloodsport

b) The Karate Kid

c) Kickboxer

d) Sidekicks

437 Which iconic '80s toy came with colorful plastic "slime" that could ooze through cages or onto action figures?

a) Masters of the Universe Slime Pit

b) Gak

c) Ooze-It

d) Creepy Crawlers

438 Which sitcom starred Tony Danza as a former baseball player who became a live-in housekeeper for a high-powered advertising executive and her family in Connecticut?

a) Family Matters

b) The Cosby Show

c) Diff'rent Strokes

d) Who's the Boss?

439 Which 1980 arcade game involved shooting down descending rows of aliens?

a) Galaga

b) Asteroids

c) Missile Command

d) Defender

440 Which fashion accessory, often neon, was worn across the forehead for workouts or aerobics?

a) Bandana

b) Headband

c) Sweatband

d) Scrunchie

FLASHBACK FACT

In 1989, Weird Al starred in the cult comedy UHF, where he dreamed up wacky TV shows like "Wheel of Fish." The movie flopped in theaters but later became a VHS favorite for superfans.

441 Which 1983 arcade game had players pilot a starfighter through the Death Star trench?

a) Star Wars Arcade
b) Space Harrier

c) Battlezone
d) Galaxian

442 Which brand of fruit drink came in shiny silver pouches with a straw you always poked wrong?

a) Capri Sun
b) Hi-C

c) Kool-Aid Bursts
d) Tang

443 Which doll, famous for her yarn hair and colorful outfit, had a horse companion named Starlite and a villain named Murky Dismal?

a) Strawberry Shortcake
b) Rainbow Brite

c) Popples
d) Care Bears

444 What 1984 comedy features a floating green glutton named Slimer, and ends with the heroes covered in marshmallow fluff after their skyscraper battle?

a) Ghostbusters
b) Gremlins

c) Poltergeist
d) Beetlejuice

445 Which flashy sneaker brand lit up the late '80s with glittery designs, high-tops, and light-up soles?

a) Reebok
b) LA Gear

c) Puma
d) Adidas

446 Which 1980s toy line featured colorful plush creatures that could tuck themselves into hidden pouches, transforming into little round bundles?

a) Popples
b) Pound Puppies

c) My Pet Monster
d) Snuggle Pets

447 Which 1980s arcade game had players racing against the clock, flying off dirt ramps, and pulling off tricky motorbike jumps on a side-scrolling track?

a) Excitebike
b) Road Rash

c) Hang-On
d) Enduro Racer

448 Which sitcom followed uptight Larry Appleton as he adjusted to life with his exuberant cousin Balki, who moved in from the fictional Mediterranean island of Mypos?

a) Who's the Boss?
b) Growing Pains

c) Silver Spoons
d) Perfect Strangers

449 Which toy line invited kids to open up miniature cases to reveal entire little worlds tucked inside?

a) Micro Machines
b) Polly Pocket

c) Littlest Pet Shop
d) Mighty Max

450 Which 1983 arcade sensation, animated by former Disney artist Don Bluth, devoured quarters as players frantically memorized joystick moves to help Dirk the Daring rescue Princess Daphne?

a) Dragon's Lair
b) Gauntlet

c) Joust
d) Altered Beast

FLASHBACK FACT

Dragon's Lair blew minds with its cartoon-like graphics. It cost 50¢ per play (double the usual price) but kids lined up anyway to watch Dirk stumble into danger.

451 Which TV host shouted "Survey says!" on Family Feud throughout the 1980s?

a) Bob Barker
b) Richard Dawson

c) Chuck Woolery
d) Pat Sajak

452 Which 1986 Tom Cruise movie featured fighter jets, volleyball, and the hit song "Danger Zone"?

a) Days of Thunder   c) Iron Eagle

b) Top Gun   d) Flight of the Intruder

453 Which teen sitcom had time-outs, neon fashion, and a gang of friends at Bayside High who always seemed to end up at The Max?

a) California Dreams   c) Saved by the Bell

b) Head of the Class   d) Parker Lewis Can't Lose

454 Which 1986 plush monster promised to be your friend, even though he was shipped wearing a pair of bright pink plastic handcuffs that kids could easily unlock?

a) Boglins   c) Madballs

b) My Pet Monster   d) Wuzzles

455 Which 1988 movie had Tom Hanks turning into an adult overnight after wishing at a fortune-telling machine?

a) Big

b) Splash

c) Bachelor Party

d) Turner & Hooch

456 Which competition show pitted everyday contestants against larger-than-life athletes with names like Nitro and Zap in events like The Joust and The Eliminator?

a) Double Dare

b) American Gladiators

c) Battle of the Stars

d) American Ninja Warrior

457 Which 1984 film starred Arnold Schwarzenegger as a cyborg assassin?

a) Predator

b) The Running Man

c) The Terminator

d) Commando

458 Which 1985 music video blew minds on MTV with its "pencil-sketch" animation and was crafted frame by frame over 16 weeks to bring a comic-book love story to life?

a) Thriller　　　　　　c) Take On Me
b) Like a Virgin　　　　d) Sweet Dreams

459 Which Nintendo boxing game featured a character named Little Mac fighting his way up the ranks?

a) Ring King　　　　　c) Heavyweight Champ
b) Punch-Out!!　　　　d) Rocky

460 Which 1988 Tim Burton classic brought to life a mischievous ghost so iconic that if you say his name three times, he just might appear?

a) Beetlejuice　　　　　　c) Ghostbusters II
b) Edward Scissorhands　　d) Poltergeist III

FLASHBACK FACT

Beetlejuice was nearly released with a much less memorable title. Warner Bros. executives pushed for the film to be called House Ghosts, and director Tim Burton jokingly suggested the alternative, Scared Sheetless, which the studio actually considered.

461 Which 1980s toy line had kids racing cars so tiny you could line up a whole "garage" on a single ruler?

a) Hot Wheels

b) Micro Machines

c) Matchbox

d) Stompers

462 Which 1984 Cyndi Lauper anthem turned up the volume on girl power and became the ultimate sing-along slumber party hit?

a) True Colors

b) Girls Just Want to Have Fun

c) Time After Time

d) She Bop

463 Which 1982 band, known for the hit song "I Ran (So Far Away), featured hairstyles that are more famous than the band?

a) A Flock of Seagulls
b) Duran Duran
c) The Cure
d) Devo

464 Which fast food chain had the slogan, "Where's the Beef?" in the mid-'80s?

a) McDonald's
b) Wendy's
c) Burger King
d) Hardee's

465 Which arcade beat-'em-up game let players clean up the streets as vigilantes Billy and Jimmy Lee?

a) Streets of Rage
b) Double Dragon
c) Final Fight
d) Renegade

466 Which 1989 sitcom started out about the Winslow family... and then got completely stolen by a cheese-loving, suspender-wearing neighbor who asked, "Did I do that?"

a) Family Matters
b) Full House
c) Perfect Strangers
d) Step by Step

467 Which soft-bodied dolls, launched in 1985, were marketed toward boys and girls as inseparable companions, even inspiring a later "Kid Sister" line?

a) My Buddy
b) Pound Puppies
c) Cabbage Patch Kids
d) Teddy Ruxpin

468 Which 1980s toy line featured futuristic warriors who carried staffs and chestplates with shimmering holograms that unlocked magical powers?

a) Visionaries
b) ThunderCats
c) SilverHawks
d) MASK

469 Which 1989 Disney film made waves by plunging under the sea and kicking off a new era of animated magic?

a) Oliver & Company

b) The Little Mermaid

c) Beauty and the Beast

d) Aladdin

470 Which 1986 Doritos flavor brought a tangy twist to snack time and made ranch... cool?

a) Nacho Cheese

b) Cool Ranch

c) Spicy Nacho

d) Salsa Verde

The Totally Rad '90s

The 1990s were all that and a bag of chips. Tamagotchis beeped in pockets, VHS tapes stacked up by the TV, and Friends, Seinfeld, and The Fresh Prince ruled living rooms. Gamers battled on Nintendo 64 and PlayStation, while music was everywhere—grunge rocked Seattle, boy bands topped the charts, and icons like Alanis Morissette gave us anthems we still shout-sing today. It was the era of dial-up internet, Blockbuster nights, and pop culture moments we'll never forget. Grab your flannel shirt, pop in a cassette, and see how well you remember the totally rad '90s!

471 Which MTV animated series followed two deadbeat teens whose "huh-huh" banter and music video commentary turned them into unexpected '90s icons?

a) Beavis and Butthead   c) The Animaniacs
b) The Simpsons   d) King of the Hill

472 What handheld digital pet had kids pressing buttons to feed, clean, and play with their pixelated companions?

a) Furby   c) Tamagotchi
b) Giga Pet   d) Digimon

473 Which sitcom gave us the phrase "How you doin'?" thanks to Joey Tribbiani?

a) Friends   c) Frasier
b) Seinfeld   d) Home Improvement

474 Which Disney film, released in 1994, had audiences singing along to "Hakuna Matata"?

a) Beauty and the Beast
b) The Little Mermaid
c) The Lion King
d) Aladdin

475 Which late '90s toy craze had collectors obsessing over heart-shaped tags and rare editions like Princess the bear?

a) Cabbage Patch Kids
b) Beanie Babies
c) Troll Dolls
d) Pound Puppies

476 Which teen drama served up love triangles, big hair, and even bigger drama at West Beverly High, making the Peach Pit the place to be?

a) Dawson's Creek
b) Beverly Hills, 90210
c) Melrose Place
d) My So-Called Life

477 Which boy band released the hit single "I Want It That Way" in 1999?

a) Backstreet Boys
b) *NSYNC

c) 98 Degrees
d) New Kids on the Block

478 Which popular sitcom followed four friends navigating life in New York, often described as "a show about nothing"?

a) Mad About You
b) Friends

c) Seinfeld
d) Dharma & Greg

479 What popular stuffed owl-like toy, launched in 1998, spoke in its own quirky language?

a) Furby
b) Giga Pet

c) Tamagotchi
d) Pound Puppy

480 Which '90s VH1 show added witty on-screen commentary and random trivia to music videos, making viewers feel like insiders with the scoop?

a) Total Request Live
b) Pop-Up Video

c) Behind the Music
d) VH1 News

FLASHBACK FACT

In the late '90s, Furby was such a craze that the NSA briefly banned them from offices, fearing the toys could "record" secret conversations. Spoiler: they couldn't.

481 Which '90s sitcom followed a bumbling DIY TV host, his often disastrous home projects, and a neighbor who offered sage advice from behind a fence?

a) Family Matters
b) Home Improvement

c) Step by Step
d) Full House

482 Which teen sitcom introduced audiences to a charismatic Philly teen whose life got flipped, turned upside down when he moved in with his wealthy relatives?

a) Moesha

b) The Fresh Prince of Bel-Air

c) Saved by the Bell

d) Hangin' with Mr. Cooper

483 Which cartoon about babies featured characters named Tommy, Chuckie, and Angelica?

a) Doug

b) Rugrats

c) Hey Arnold!

d) Rocket Power

484 Which actress shot to international stardom after starring in the 1997 epic about a doomed ocean liner and a very famous door?

a) Julia Roberts

b) Kate Winslet

c) Cameron Diaz

d) Sandra Bullock

485 What fruity snack had kids obsessed with its liquid center when you bit into it?

a) Fruit Roll-Ups

c) Gushers

b) Dunkaroos

d) Fruit by the Foot

486 Which NBA star earned his nickname because he "always delivered," becoming one of the most consistent scorers of the 1990s?

a) Karl Malone

c) Hakeem Olajuwon

b) Charles Barkley

d) Patrick Ewing

487 What 1999 sci-fi film had Keanu Reeves dodging bullets in slow motion?

a) The Matrix

c) Johnny Mnemonic

b) Dark City

d) Blade

488 Which British girl group dominated '90s pop with nicknames like Sporty, Scary, and Baby?

a) Destiny's Child   c) Spice Girls
b) TLC   d) All Saints

489 What Nickelodeon game show had kids climbing the Aggro Crag?

a) Double Dare   c) GUTS
b) Legends of the   d) Wild & Crazy Kids
Hidden Temple

490 Which mid-'90s website revolutionized garage sales by taking bidding wars online, whether you wanted vintage toys, rare collectibles, or someone's old toaster?

a) eBay   c) Yahoo!
b) Amazon   d) Craigslist

FLASHBACK FACT

Before streaming took over, Blockbuster was the weekend destination. You'd roam the aisles for the perfect VHS, grab some popcorn at checkout, and hope the last renter remembered to "Be Kind, Rewind." Forgetting could cost you a fee, or worse, a judgmental look from the clerk.

491 Which '90s cult-favorite TV show followed a California teen chosen to battle the forces of darkness while still navigating crushes, homework, and high school?

a) Charmed
b) Buffy the Vampire Slayer

c) Sabrina the Teenage Witch
d) Dawson's Creek

492 Which 1990s cartoon starred two lab mice – one a genius, the other not so much – who plotted to take over the world every night?

a) Pinky and the Brain
b) Freakazoid!

c) Tiny Toon Adventures
d) Rocko's Modern Life

493 Who was the first woman to win the U.S. figure skating gold medal since Dorothy Hamill, in 1998?

a) Tara Lipinski   c) Michelle Kwan
b) Nancy Kerrigan   d) Tonya Harding

494 Which '90s sitcom followed a sophisticated radio psychiatrist starting a new life in Seattle, complete with sibling banter, a neurotic producer, and one very good dog?

a) Friends   c) Frasier
b) Cheers   d) Caroline in the City

495 Which animated MTV series followed a teen with round glasses, combat boots, and a razor-sharp wit as she navigated the absurd world of high school in Lawndale?

a) Daria   c) Doug
b) Beavis and Butt-Head   d) The Critic

496 Which Canadian singer released the 1995 album Jagged Little Pill, including hits like "Ironic" and "Hand in my Pocket"?

a) Celine Dion

b) Shania Twain

c) Alanis Morissette

d) Sarah McLachlan

497 Which animated Disney film featured the voice of Robin Williams as a genie?

a) Mulan

b) Aladdin

c) Hercules

d) Tarzan

498 Which 1996 holiday toy craze had parents camping out overnight and caused stampedes in stores as everyone tried to snag the giggling, red sensation?

a) Furby

b) Beanie Babies

c) Tickle Me Elmo

d) Tamagotchi

499 Which actor lent his voice to the space ranger with a catchphrase about going "to infinity and beyond" in Pixar's Toy Story?

a) Tom Hanks

b) Tim Allen

c) Billy Crystal

d) Robin Williams

500 Which 1999 teen rom-com had Freddie Prinze Jr. betting he could turn an artsy, glasses-wearing classmate into prom queen?

a) Clueless

b) Can't Hardly Wait

c) She's All That

d) 10 Things I Hate About You

FLASHBACK FACT

Before Jagged Little Pill, Alanis Morissette was a teen dance-pop star in Canada. Her 1991 debut album Alanis went platinum in Canada, earning her a Juno Award at just 18. She was even dubbed "Canada's Debbie Gibson" and opened for Vanilla Ice!

Bonus Blitz

You've jitterbugged through the '40s, cruised the sock hops of the '50s, twirled through the Summer of Love, moonwalked through the '80s, and survived the screech of dial-up internet. Now it's time for the ultimate throwback challenge: a grab bag of questions from every corner of the nostalgic universe.

These questions don't belong to any single decade, they're here to keep you on your toes. Think of this as your fun encore!

SCORING

The Bonus Blitz isn't part of your official decade scores, it's just for bragging rights. You can keep it casual, or if you'd like a little extra challenge, use this mini scale:

- ◆ 10–12 correct: **Bonus Blitz Master**
- ◆ 7–9 correct: **Retro Whiz**
- ◆ 4–6 correct: **Memory Lane Explorer**
- ◆ 0–3 correct: **Casual Time Traveler**

Have fun and see how deep your nostalgic brain really goes!

Which 1957 Dr. Seuss book featured a cat in a striped hat who brought chaos to a rainy afternoon?

a) Green Eggs and Ham
b) The Cat in the Hat
c) Horton Hears a Who!
d) How the Grinch Stole Christmas

Which 1970s variety show featured a singing and dancing family who got their start with a bubblegum hit about a puppy?

a) The Partridge Family
b) The Jackson 5ive
c) The Osmonds
d) The Brady Bunch Variety Hour

Which 1982 Steven Spielberg film terrified kids and adults alike with a possessed TV set and the warning "They're here"?

a) Gremlins
b) Poltergeist
c) The Thing
d) Twilight Zone: The Movie

Which 1940s radio show followed the adventures of a masked vigilante and his faithful companion Tonto?

a) The Shadow
b) The Lone Ranger

c) The Green Hornet
d) Superman

Which 1990s Nickelodeon cartoon followed a football-headed kid navigating life in the city with his best friend Gerald?

a) Doug
b) Rocket Power

c) Hey Arnold!
d) CatDog

Which 1960s board game had players spinning their way through college, careers, paydays, and taxes?

a) The Game of Life
b) Payday

c) Careers
d) Rich Uncle

Which 1987 Patrick Swayze film had audiences quoting "Nobody puts Baby in a corner"?

a) Road House
b) Dirty Dancing
c) Ghost
d) Red Dawn

Which 1950s horror host, dressed in black and known for her witty commentary, introduced B-movies on late-night TV?

a) Vampira
b) Elvira
c) Morticia
d) Lily Munster

Which 1970s Charlie's Angels star became a fashion icon thanks to her famous feathered hairstyle that everyone wanted to copy?

a) Kate Jackson
b) Jaclyn Smith
c) Cheryl Ladd
d) Farrah Fawcett

Which 1990s coffee chain exploded across America, making lattes and Frappuccinos part of everyday life?

a) Starbucks
b) Dunkin' Donuts

c) Peet's Coffee
d) The Coffee Bean

Which 1960s TV Western followed the adventures of the Ponderosa ranch family and ran for 14 seasons?

a) Gunsmoke
b) Bonanza

c) Rawhide
d) The Rifleman

Which 1980s breakfast cereal featured a rabbit who was always chasing after kids' bowls while they chanted "Silly rabbit..."?

a) Cocoa Puffs
b) Lucky Charms

c) Trix
d) Fruity Pebbles

1940s ANSWER KEY

1. Milton Berle
2. Coca Cola
3. Casablanca
4. Clue
5. Swing
6. Captain America
7. Harry S. Truman
8. It's a Wonderful Life
9. Cheetos
10. Slinky
11. Dizzy Gillespie
12. Double Indemnity
13. Brylcreem
14. Rosie the Riveter
15. Robin
16. Hiroshima
17. V-Mail (Victory Mail)
18. Utility fashion
19. Glenn Miller
20. United Nations

21. Charlie Chaplin
22. Edith Piaf
23. Tupperware
24. Oklahoma!
25. Polaroid
26. 33 1/3 RPM LP Record
27. Lucky Strike
28. South Pacific
29. Jackie Robinson
30. CBS

1950s ANSWER KEY

31. I Love Lucy

32. Elvis Presley

33. Hula Hoop

34. Don Larsen

35. No-Cal

36. Sputnik 1

37. Ford

38. Lady and the Tramp

39. McDonald's

40. Kidney

41. James Dean

42. Dick Clark

43. Joe DiMaggio

44. Blackboard Jungle

45. Grace Kelly

46. Mr. Potato Head

47. Willie Mays

48. Southdale Center

49. Jane Russell

50. The King and I

51. You Bet Your Life

52. Abbott and Costello

53. Pepsi

54. The Mickey Mouse Club

55. Charlie Brown

56. The vertical grille that many critics compared to a toilet seat or a horse collar.

57. Twenty-One

58. The structure of DNA

59. Disneyland

60. Poodle skirts

61. Risk

62. 7-Up

63. Marilyn Monroe

64. The pompadour

65. Porky Pig

66. Mickey Mantle

67. Hostess CupCakes

68. Squirt gun

69. Silly Putty

1950s ANSWER KEY

70. Buddy Holly

71. Leather jacket

72. Mattel

73. The Untouchables

74. Perry Como

75. Cadillac Eldorado

76. Ding Dong School

77. M&Ms

78. Beetle Bailey

79. Charlton Heston

80. Dodgers

81. Jonas Salk

82. Cracker Jack

83. Ralph Edwards

84. KFC

85. Lawrence Welk

86. Rocky Marciano

87. Colorforms

88. Dennis the Menace

89. Althea Gibson

90. Betty Crocker

91. The Music Man

92. Wonder Bread

93. Lassie

94. Hershey's Kisses

95. Corning Ware

96. Vincent Price

97. The Creature from the Black Lagoon

98. Varsity letters

99. Nat King Cole

100. Swanson TV Dinners

101. 16 Magazine

102. Ben-Hur

103. Rosa Parks

104. Alfred Hitchcock

105. NASA

106. Alaska & Hawaii

107. Play-Doh

108. Elvis Presley

109. Federal-Aid Highway Act

1950s ANSWER KEY

110. Frisbee

111. A plane crash that killed Buddy Holly, Ritchie Valens, and J.P. "The Big Bopper" Richardson

112. Diners Club

113. Clothes dryer

114. Spy Pen

115. Levittown

116. Linus

117. Wooly Willy

118. Roman Holiday

119. Life Savers

120. Pick-Up Sticks

121. The pin curl

122. How the Grinch Stole Christmas

123. The Wild One

124. Bus driver

125. Johnny Mathis

126. Saddle shoes

127. Betty Cooper

128. To Catch a Thief

129. Milk Duds

130. The Howdy Doody Show

131. Matchbox

132. White Christmas

133. Zenith Space Command

134. Bobby Day

135. Easy-Off Oven Cleaner

136. Godzilla

137. Bonanza

138. Necco Wafers

139. Sweet Smell of Success

140. Coonskin cap

141. Jimi Hendrix

142. The Love Bug

143. Lucky Charms

144. Operation

145. Audrey Hepburn

146. Pontiac

147. Where the Wild Things Are

1960s ANSWER KEY

148. Rudolph the Red-Nosed Reindeer

149. Bonnie and Clyde

150. Woodstock

151. Easy-Bake Oven

152. Dr. No

153. Batman

154. Pop-Tarts

155. Apollo 11

156. The Supremes

157. Froot Loops

158. The Jetsons

159. The Sound of Music

160. G.I. Joe

161. Haight-Ashbury gatherings

162. Twiggy

163. 2001: A Space Odyssey

164. Peter, Paul and Mary

165. I Dream of Jeannie

166. 101 Dalmatians

167. Muhammad Ali

168. Doritos

169. Mister Ed

170. Chevrolet Impala

171. Star Trek

172. Jim Nabors

173. Rosemary's Baby

174. Coca-Cola

175. In the Heat of the Night

176. Spirograph

177. Bullitt

178. The Andy Griffith Show

179. John Glenn

180. Hair

181. The Birds

182. Scooby-Doo, Where Are You!

183. Led Zeppelin

184. Guess Who's Coming to Dinner

185. Ding Dongs

1960s ANSWER KEY

186. The Howdy Doody Show

187. Lyndon B. Johnson

188. Butch Cassidy and the Sundance Kid

189. The Sassoon

190. Rock 'Em Sock 'Em Robots

191. Encyclopedia Brown

192. The Graduate

193. Mary Quant

194. The Good, the Bad and the Ugly

195. Psycho

196. The Alan Brady Show

197. Robot Commando

198. The Great Escape

199. True Grit

200. Cosmopolitan

201. The Carol Burnett Show

202. The Twist

203. A Hard Day's Night

204. Starburst

205. The Odd Couple

206. Cap'n Crunch

207. Cleopatra

208. Super Ball

209. Cool Hand Luke

210. Goldfinger

211. Easy Rider

212. Let's Make a Deal

213. Doctor Zhivago

214. Planet of the Apes

215. Tie-dye

216. Ocean's 11

217. Night of the Living Dead

218. Funny Girl

219. Lemonhead

220. Bewitched

221. Pet Sounds

222. Lava Lamp

223. My Mother the Car

1960s ANSWER KEY

224. "Make Love, Not War"

225. Barrel of Monkeys

226. Aretha Franklin

227. The Flintstones

228. Hippie necklaces

229. Charade

230. Ho Hos

231. The Jerk

232. "Sock it to me!"

233. The Munsters

234. Be My Baby

235. Creepy Crawlers

236. The Flying Nun

237. The Beehive

238. Twister

239. Bob Dylan

240. Mary Poppins

241. Trouble

242. My Favorite Martian

243. (I Can't Get No) Satisfaction

244. James Brown

245. Etch A Sketch

246. Flipper

247. Nik-L-Nip

248. Herman's Hermits

249. Hello, Dolly!

250. The Evil of Frankenstein

1970s ANSWER KEY

251. A Chorus Line

252. Happy Days

253. Stayin' Alive

254. The Bicentennial

255. Pong

256. Atari 2600

257. The Brady Bunch

258. Pink Floyd

259. Skylab

260. Grease

261. The Muppet Movie

262. Pet Rock

263. Jaws

264. Gerald Ford

265. Bridge Over Troubled Water

266. Walkman

267. Roots

268. Disco

269. Saturday Night Live

270. Willy Wonka & the Chocolate Factory

271. Voyager 1

272. Rocky

273. Mood ring

274. The Godfather

275. Dodge Challenger

276. SeaWorld Orlando

277. Roller skating

278. Alien

279. Oil embargo

280. Bohemian Rhapsody

281. Simon

282. CB radio boom

283. Rumours

284. Taxi Driver

285. Breakout

286. Young Frankenstein

287. Apple II

288. Three Mile Island

289. Pop Rocks

290. Wonder Woman

1970s ANSWER KEY

291. Dungeons & Dragons

292. Farrah Fawcett

293. Title IX

294. The Jeffersons

295. Halloween

296. Born to Run

297. Monty Python and the Holy Grail

298. Concorde

299. Asteroids

300. Schoolhouse Rock!

301. Maude

302. The Eagles

303. Glacier

304. The Jerk

305. Ramones

306. Mad Max

307. Voyager

308. Kung Fu Fighting

309. Laverne & Shirley

310. Star Wars

311. Garfield

312. Andy Warhol

313. The Electric Company

314. Studio 54

315. The Exorcist

316. Three's Company

317. Stairway to Heaven

318. Close Encounters of the Third Kind

319. King Kong

320. I Will Survive

321. Sanford and Son

322. Centennial

323. Superman

324. Songs in the Key of Life

325. Space Invaders

326. Soylent Green

327. The Gong Show

328. Carole King

329. Magnavox Odyssey

330. The Towering Inferno

1970s ANSWER KEY

331. Washington: Behind Closed Doors

332. The Jeffersons

333. USA vs. USSR

334. Life of Brian

335. All the President's Men

336. Twix

337. The Village People

338. Are You There God? It's Me, Margaret

339. Hank Aaron

340. The Wiz

341. Carrie

342. M*A*S*H*

343. Meatballs

344. Tommy

345. Good Times

346. I Feel Love

347. Network

348. The Poseidon Adventure

349. Strawberry Shortcake

350. Rich Man, Poor Man

351. Connections

352. The Mary Tyler Moore Show

353. Killing Me Softly with His Song

354. Le Freak

355. Apollo 13

356. I Will Always Love You

357. Battlestar Galactica

358. Amazing Grace

359. One Flew Over the Cuckoo's Nest

360. Mork & Mindy

1980s ANSWER KEY

361. Alf

362. Pac-Man

363. Trapper Keeper

364. Donkey Kong

365. Big League Chew

366. Jellies

367. Cabbage Patch Kids

368. Punky Brewster

369. Swatch Watch

370. Garbage Pail Kids

371. Duck Hunt

372. Super Mario Bros.

373. Talking Whiz Kid

374. Slouch socks

375. Gremlins

376. MTV

377. Double Dare

378. Tetris

379. High-tops

380. Care Bears

381. Press Your Luck

382. Ms. Pac-Man

383. Kool-Aid

384. My Little Pony

385. Atari 5200

386. Trivial Pursuit

387. Gizmo

388. The Goonies

389. Tiger Electronics

390. Don't Stop Believin'

391. Rubik's Cube

392. Koosh Ball

393. You Can't Do That on Television

394. Knight Rider

395. Madballs

396. Tempest

397. The Joy of Painting

398. The Legend of Zelda

399. The Breakfast Club

400. Transformers

1980s ANSWER KEY

401. Michael Jordan

402. "Weird Al" Yankovic

403. Dig Dug

404. Fruit Roll-Ups

405. Thundercats

406. Wargames

407. Big Red

408. M.U.S.C.L.E.

409. The Golden Girls

410. Jellies

411. Speak & Spell

412. Family Ties

413. Skip-It

414. Frogger

415. Teddy Ruxpin

416. Book It!

417. Reebok Pump

418. E.T. the Extra-Terrestrial

419. Friendship Pins

420. Back to the Future

421. Rainbow Brite

422. Nintendo Entertainment System (NES)

423. Labyrinth

424. Hubba Bubba

425. Doozers

426. Wacky Wall Walkers

427. Q*bert

428. Scrunchie

429. McDonald's

430. Alex Kidd

431. Pound Puppies

432. Full House

433. Slap Bracelets

434. Slip 'N Slide

435. Charles in Charge

436. The Karate Kid

437. Masters of the Universe Slime Pit

438. Who's the Boss?

439. Galaga

1980s ANSWER KEY

440. Headband

441. Star Wars Arcade

442. Capri Sun

443. Rainbow Brite

444. Ghostbusters

445. LA Gear

446. Popples

447. Excitebike

448. Perfect Strangers

449. Polly Pocket

450. Dragon's Lair

451. Richard Dawson

452. Top Gun

453. Saved by the Bell

454. My Pet Monster

455. Big

456. American Gladiators

457. The Terminator

458. Take On Me

459. Punch-Out!!

460. Beetlejuice

461. Micro Machines

462. Girls Just Want to Have Fun

463. A Flock of Seagulls

464. Wendy's

465. Double Dragon

466. Family Matters

467. My Buddy

468. Visionaries

469. The Little Mermaid

470. Cool Ranch Doritos

1990s ANSWER KEY

471. Beavis and Butthead

472. Tamagotchi

473. Friends

474. The Lion King

475. Beanie Babies

476. Beverly Hills, 90210

477. Backstreet Boys

478. Seinfeld

479. Furby

480. Pop-Up Video

481. Home Improvement

482. The Fresh Prince of Bel-Air

483. Rugrats

484. Kate Winslet

485. Gushers

486. Karl Malone

487. The Matrix

488. Spice Girls

489. GUTS

490. eBay

491. Buffy the Vampire Slayer

492. Pinky and the Brain

493. Tara Lipinski

494. Frasier

495. Daria

496. Alanis Morissette

497. Aladdin

498. Tickle Me Elmo

499. Tim Allen

500. She's All That

Bonus Blitz ANSWER KEY

The Cat in the Hat

The Osmonds

Poltergeist

The Lone Ranger

Hey Arnold!

The Game of Life

Dirty Dancing

Vampira

Farrah Fawcett

Starbucks

Bonanza

Trix

Copyright © 2025 Practical Use Publishing.

All rights reserved.

No part of this book may be reproduced or distributed without prior written permission, except for brief quotations in reviews or uses allowed by law.

ISBN: 979-8-9917595-9-5

Printed in the United States of America.

bit.ly/clarknewbook

www.ingramcontent.com/pod-product-compliance
Lightning Source LLC
Chambersburg PA
CBHW072139090426
42739CB00013B/3224